4/10/22

The Pet Loss Guide

The Pet Loss Guide

MILLIE JACOBS

First published in Great Britain in 2022 by Orion Spring
an imprint of The Orion Publishing Group Ltd
Carmelite House, 50 Victoria Embankment
London EC4Y 0DZ

An Hachette UK Company

1 3 5 7 9 10 8 6 4 2

A CIP catalogue record for this book is
available from the British Library.

ISBN (Hardback) 978 1 4091 9592 4
ISBN (eBook) 978 1 4091 9593 1

Typeset by Input Data Services Ltd, Somerset

Printed and bound in Great Britain by Clays Ltd, Elcograf S.p.A.

ORION
SPRING

www.orionbooks.co.uk

Contents

The Power of the Dog

There is sorrow enough in the natural way
From men and women to fill our day;
And when we are certain of sorrow in store,
Why do we always arrange for more?
Brothers and Sisters, I bid you beware
Of giving your heart to a dog to tear.

Buy a pup and your money will buy
Love unflinching that cannot lie –
Perfect passion and worship fed
By a kick in the ribs or a pat on the head.
Nevertheless, it is hardly fair
To risk your heart for a dog to tear.

When the fourteen years which Nature permits
Are closing in asthma, or tumour, or fits,
And the vet's unspoken prescription runs
To lethal chambers or loaded guns,
Then you will find – it's your own affair –
But . . . you've given your heart to a dog to tear.

When the body that lived at your single will,
With its whimper of welcome, is stilled (how still!),
When the spirit that answered your every mood
Is gone – wherever it goes – for good,
You will discover how much you care,
And will give your heart to a dog to tear.

We've sorrow enough in the natural way,
When it comes to burying Christian clay.
Our loves are not given, but only lent,
At compound interest of cent per cent.
Though it is not always the case, I believe,
That the longer we've kept 'em, the more do we grieve:
For, when debts are payable, right or wrong,
A short-time loan is as bad as a long –
So why in – Heaven (before we are there)
Should we give our hearts to a dog to tear?

Rudyard Kipling

Introduction

Iimagine that you will be picking up this book because you have lost a beloved pet, and my heart goes out to you. Let me begin by saying I don't think anyone should write a book like this unless they have lost a pet themselves, and know that heartbreaking grief. I can share that I have lost many pets over the years, and each one broke me.

My love of animals started as a child. I don't remember when we didn't have a dog in the family, and they were considered family members; yes, they had four legs, but they were valued, loved and cherished.

The first dog I remember was called Lassie. My parents had found her abandoned on the motorway. We then had a dog named Kerry-Gold. We had Kerry as a puppy, and we didn't say goodbye to her until I was an adult. Along with Kerry, we then got another rescue dog named Ross, and he and Kerry lived happily together for over 10 years.

When I got married, having a dog seemed an obvious thing to do, but we knew it was utterly impractical due to us travelling so much with work, so we put it off. One day we were driving somewhere and we came across a stray dog who was starving to death. We got him into our car and took him to the local rescue kennels. The following day, my mum spoke to a vet and told her that we had found a dog and where we had taken it. The vet said to her that those kennels had a terrible reputation and we should go and ask for the dog back. The moment I was told, I leapt into my car, drove to the kennels and asked for him back. I saw the cage they had put him in, and there was hardly room for him to even turn around. I filled out all the necessary paperwork and took his lead.

Within days, Jake ruled our home. He ignored every rule we tried to enforce – not getting on the sofa etc. – and while we knew having a dog was going to be hard work, our house suddenly felt like home.

Jake was like a human in the body of a dog: he had a sense of humour, he was wild, took risks (for instance, if he saw an open window, he would leap out of it and take himself for a walk), but he also showed us such love. We had him for 12 years, and the day he died still haunts me.

Jake had a couple of strokes and a chronic bout of pancreatitis. Each of these illnesses made him even more dependent on us, and I guess us on him. We changed our work hours; we even stopped travelling internationally, as we didn't want to leave his side. Life really did revolve around Jake's needs. We never resented these changes, because we loved him so much and were happy to work around his requirements. But as he became the main focus of our world, it shook our existence when he died.

The Day We Said Goodbye

Jake had another stroke while we were staying at my parents' house in the South West. We found a vet near to their house, and she told us that Jake could make a full recovery. A week later he was so much better and we felt he was ready for us to travel home. We made an appointment with our own vet, as we had a great relationship with him, and he had known Jake since we homed him. After examining him and taking blood, the vet said he looked fine and, hopefully, the blood tests would confirm that all was now well. We went home very relieved. A few hours later, though, we took Jake into the garden, and it was clear something wasn't right. He partly collapsed and needed assistance to get in the house. We called the vet and begged him to do a house call, but he said he would need to see him at the surgery in case he needed to operate, so we should get him there as fast as possible. We carried him into the car and I sat in the back with him; he laid his head on my knee. I could see the pain in his eyes. That 20-minute car ride felt like hours.

My husband carried him into the surgery and the vet led us through to a consulting room. He listened to Jake's chest and then said to us, 'This is the end. We need to put him to sleep immediately; if we don't, he will have a heart attack in front of you.' We told him to give Jake the injection, as we didn't want him to have an ounce more pain. We lay with him as the injection was administered, and we felt his heart stop beating. The vet asked if we'd like him to arrange for Jake's cremation and we agreed.

The next few hours are vague and torturous to remember. We walked out of the surgery numb, dazed, in shock and devastated. We didn't want to go straight home, so we went to my grandparents to tell them what had happened ... but we knew at some point we would need to return to our house. As we walked in, we saw Jake's bed, his toys ... his presence was everywhere, and the pain was beyond horrific.

We went to bed sobbing, and the next day decided we couldn't stay in the house any longer. We packed a bag, got in the car and started to drive. We ended up going from England all the way to the top of Scotland ... crying all the way.

To this day, I don't know if Jake dying was the straw that broke the camel's back or whether I would still have responded in this way even if I hadn't already encountered such extreme loss in the past, of both people and pets, but it definitely broke me. Life felt pointless, hopeless and devoid of light.

After days and days of driving, we decided that we needed to go back, as we knew we would need to collect Jake's ashes from the vet. Walking back through our front door was horrendous: his bed was still there, his toys were still there, but the house was still silent. No little dog footsteps. No barks. Our house no longer felt like a home, it felt like just a house, and we hated being in it.

That raw, dark pain lasted a few months, and we decided the only way for us even to like our house again was to find another dog that needed rescuing. Not a replacement dog, as that would never be possible, but another dog we could love and take care of. We eventually found a beautiful spaniel who was in a foster home, having been found at a puppy farm. It took me a few weeks to love her, as I was so worried anyone might think we were 'replacing' Jake, but after a little time I realised I could love them both; and by rescuing this little dog, it felt like we were doing something in Jake's honour.

'How it is that animals understand things I do not know, but it is certain that they do understand. Perhaps there is a language which is not made of words and everything in the world understands it. Perhaps there is a soul hidden in everything and it can always speak, without even making a sound, to another soul.'

Frances Hodgson Burnett

This book is laid out in four chapters: the grief journey; advice for dealing with practical issues; advice for how to support someone who is grieving for a pet; and a final brief chapter on healing and happiness. Then there are two sections at the back of the book, the first dealing with questions I'm often asked, and the second a guide to how to handle the first month of bereavement. There's space there to write down your feelings, or why not start keeping a journal and adding to that daily? It's a very effective way of processing your grief, and I would urge you to keep one.

Grief can make you feel so alone, but the feelings you are currently encountering will be being felt by so many others. I asked people to share their stories of pet loss with me, so I could include them in this book. I hope their stories will show you that the grief from losing a pet can be as real and profound as when losing a person, and that no one should be ashamed of the feelings they encounter when navigating the loss of their beloved companion.

Tinker

I suppose it's not uncommon, as a young adult, to be called home to say goodbye to a childhood pet, perhaps to attend a euthanasia or a backyard burial, sharing stories and shedding tears. This is a sobering experience, but it's one that comes to pass much like a rite of passage. Aside from their longevity that typically spans three decades, most horse–human relationships are complex and intricate. They are thousand-pound beasts that we trust to carry us safely, perform when asked, to move forward with light touches. They trust us to feed them, to care for them. To ride upon their backs. They are, most often, docile, obedient creatures. They are friends; they are partners.

So, when I found myself on the receiving end of the call that announced the grim news – 'We're euthanising Tinker tomorrow' – I wasn't expecting the enormity of emotions and memories that would come flooding back. After all, I was in my thirties, married with children, and Tinker had (for all intents and purposes) been my parents' horse for the second half of her life. She had been ailing for quite some time, and the news was not unexpected. 'Of course,' I said. 'I'll be there.'

As a vet tech and a girl who grew up on a horse farm, euthanasia was nothing new to me. It was something I viewed as a kindness, as a way to end suffering before dignity was lost. I packed up my three-year-old, figuring she really wouldn't know what was happening, and headed home the next day.

It was when I arrived that it really hit me. My dad had told me that 'everyone' would be there, but I wasn't prepared for the small crowd that was milling about in the driveway, smiling and chatting despite the solemn air. Our *barn friends*, we'd called them, the women who'd taught me how to ride and the men who'd purchased pick-up trucks and trailers for their wives to drive us to horse shows. The vet was already there, and in the distance I saw the yellow flash of the backhoe that had prepared a grave. This was really happening.

Someone took my daughter, and I went to the paddock to say goodbye. My mom was there, and she looked as shaken and pale as one might expect . . . after all, this was her first horse. This was the one who'd actualised her child-hood dreams of owning horses. This was the one whom our farm was named after, the one I'd been 'forced' to ride because *this is the horse we have*. The one I had learned on, who received compliments on her beauty everywhere we went. The one who had put up with my nonsense as a young, inexperienced rider and who had unequivocally been a part of my life for as long as I could remember. She was easily equated with home.

My goodbyes were surreal, over and done within moments . . . everyone was waiting. This wasn't a simple administration of drugs to a vein, and I found myself feel-ing foolish that I thought it would be so. It was a leading of Tinker away from our other horse, her daughter Annie, who had not been separated from her in 15 years. It was the death march, the plank walk, the last turnout as my mother led her to the giant hole in the ground. It was the other bodies standing around her, ready to make the fall as gentle as they could. It was the end of the road, and when the sedative hit and she went down, part of us went down with her.

I burst into tears, my daughter's stroller turned away from the field to shield her, and the woman who'd first lifted me up onto a pony when I was just seven years old held me. I wanted to watch, to keep my eyes on my mother, but I couldn't. I was overcome with sobs, the embarrassing, wracking kind, completely dumbfounded as to how this part of my childhood – of my whole life – was already over. I snuck glances at my daughter, who was happily playing with her toys, and felt the sorrowful knowledge that she would never really know Tinker.

If it sounds gut-wrenching, it got worse. The soundtrack to this moment, to this colossal death, was the frantic whinnying of Annie, Tinker's daughter. The consensus, once the vet confirmed that Tinker had passed, was to let Annie out to see her before the grisly work of burial began.

Annie, a carbon copy of her mother, a shining bay with a big white star, galloped out into the field. She did several laps around the body, the backhoe, the hole and the people that were intruding on her pasture. She eventually wound her concentric circles down and spent a few moments sniffing Tinker and then – just like that – she was done. In the way that animals do, a way that we humans can never quite master, Annie accepted the death for what it was.

We eventually made our way back to the kitchen, save for those who remained to do the final duties. The familiar and distinct laughs of the women began to fill the air as we all talked, caught up, broke bread and shared stories and memories. There was a nostalgia that rose heavy on that day, like smoke lingering long after the fire had burnt out.

A horse is a friend who trusts you more than it should. A willing servant, often a gentle giant and, just as there is a massive presence in life, there is a massive presence in death as well. The immenseness of the mourning and the subsequent quiet acceptance teaches us that there is beauty even in the most sorrowful of times.

And my daughter? The three-year-old I regretted bringing along, not realising the gravity of the situation? The one that I lamented would never know Tinker? *She* remembers all of that day, astonishingly. But her descriptions are different from ours. I think of anguish, I think of how I sobbed, how heartbroken my parents were. My daughter?

'It's the day Tinker went to heaven,' she became fond of saying, 'in the pasture so she is always with Annie.'

1

The Grief Journey

The animals we share our lives with are not 'just pets'. They are friends, life companions, even soul mates. It feels as if they 'know' things about us, they sense our moods, they wordlessly seem to know what we need. We build our routines, our work and our lives around them. They give us joy, love, often purpose. They also teach us about devotion and loyalty. These precious souls give us so much, and when they die it can feel like a part of us also dies.

What I would love this book to do for you is to help you see the value of grief in all of our lives, wherever the grief may be born from, and for the words within its pages to teach you to accept its place rather than fight it. If we give grief a chair around our table, it stops it constantly knocking on our door without invitation. We need to see that grief doesn't have to be a monster living under the bed; it can be a companion we don't need to run from. When we can see pain and grief like this, it lessens the grip it has on our lives.

One of the things I have learned on my journey is that the way we view grief and loss depends on our personal views of death and life. If we value every living creature, whether their life be short or long, that changes how we grieve and – importantly – how we live. If we want to embrace life, we also need to accept death; the two go hand in hand, and if we can lose the fear surrounding this often-taboo subject, we become more able to deal with the emotions that grief and loss bring.

The grief from losing an animal is not a different type or form of grief – grief is grief! So, whether you lose a person, a home, financial security, a job, relationship or your beloved pet, you are dealing with the same emotions and have to process the loss to enable you to move forwards healthily.

Nitro

'Nitro, domestic short hair, white and grey, male', the little white piece of paper on the side of the cage read. A 40-minute drive in early November 2001 with my mother to the humane society in our neighbouring town led me to the outside of this little kitten's cage. Two white and grey paws reached through the bars, grasping, begging for some attention. A little white face with a dirty grey nose and eyes that looked as if they contained the galaxy cried out to us.

The little 10-year-old girl staring back at him could never imagine this little kitten would become her best friend and confidant for nearly 19 years.

This cat was made different, and I mean different. A white cat with large grey spots, a permanent butt-waddle since his hind end was comically higher than his front, and a tail that was always curled over his back in a circle. He was built different. And he didn't meow like any other cat. His vocalisations were more squeaks, grunts and his signature chortle, 'Ureeeee!'

Nitro was there for me every day after elementary school. We would play in the backyard, go for walks around the block and make our way to his favourite park a block from our house where he would seek out his special tree that grew catnip around the base. After eating and enjoying his fill we would walk back home, where I would sit cross-legged on the couch as he would curl up and purr on my lap when I worked on my homework or watched TV with my mother after supper.

Nitro was always there, he just became a part of my everyday life. The first thing I did each day was go inside our house and say hi to Nitro. He was there for all the high school adjustments, drama and difficult study sessions. There for college courses, projects, late nights and early mornings.

After graduating college, I moved about an hour away, but would still come home every chance I could to visit my mother, her cats, and especially Nitro. Each time, without fail, I was treated with a familiar 'Ureeeee!'

Through the years I switched jobs, switched apartments, and my boyfriend became my husband. Our apartment living turned into home ownership, our joys and celebrations of becoming pregnant led to sorrow as our first baby was suddenly gone at the end of the first trimester.

Through joy and success, trauma and sorrow, Nitro was my steady ground. A constant in an ever-changing world, I could always count on him being there every time I walked into my mother's home.

In October 2020, knowing Nitro hadn't got much time left, I made the hour drive to my mother's home, hoping and wishing that Nitro would still be alive when I got there. As I walked into my childhood home I was treated by a familiar chortle: 'Ureee.' A little quieter and raspy this time.

Nitro was curled up in his little bed, basking in the autumn sun in his favourite window. His coat was thin and sparse, his muscles stiff, his galaxy eyes sunken in but still so full of happiness.

We did everything that day. He ate his favourite foods, lay in the grass, and tried so hard to get to the park for his favourite treat, fresh-grown catnip. As we came to the end of the block he stopped and looked back at me, beckoning me to carry him across the road. I scooped up his frail little body and we made our way to his tree, the one with catnip at the base.

I spent the rest of the evening sleeping on the floor with Nitro's bed right beside my pillow. As the evening turned into night Nitro's life began to fade. His responses were slower, his mind was drifting, and his breathing began to change. Throughout the night I checked his responses, administered medication and talked with him about all the good years we'd had together.

By early morning he was in a coma-like state. This was it. My lifeline was leaving me. For a few hours I watched his chest rise and fall as he took fewer and fewer breaths; I told him I loved him and that it was okay to go. I told him to cross that rainbow bridge, start his new chapter.

In his last moment his frail little paw clenched tightly around my fingers. He took a ragged breath and as the air left his lungs I felt each of his claws retract from my hand and his paw relax.

He was gone. I scooped up his frail body and cradled him, memorising his every marking, not believing that I would never hear his chortle again.

After an hour or so I cleaned him up and laid him out, curled up in his favourite bed, ready for his burial later that evening.

I dug his grave at the base of a large elm tree in the backyard. As I lowered his blanket-wrapped body into that hole it felt as if my heart was being sucked out of my chest. I kept saying over and over that I didn't want to let go. I didn't want to stop touching him, I couldn't comprehend this little kitten that had come into my life nearly 19 years earlier, this cat who would greet me every time I went home, this good old boy who I could always tell my excitements, troubles, and traumas to was gone.

The dirt felt cold as it ran through my fingers. Every scoop that covered Nitro drew a ragged painful breath from my throat. As I smoothed out the dirt I sat back and wept. I felt so empty, so alone. Like a piece of myself was under that black dirt.

The deaths of all my previous pets had left me with a heart-wrenching grief, and unexplainable pain. But losing Nitro caused a very unique pain; it felt as if each fibre in my body was being unravelled. I was left holding all the loose threads from what was left of my heart.

I still imitate his chortle from time to time, and each time now it brings a smile to my face and puts back a stitch in my heart. The pain of losing him has transformed into precious memories. I still cry for him. I still miss him terribly. Visiting his grave always brings me back down to my knees and steals tears from my eyes. But I thank him each time I think of him. I thank him for being my constant non-judging companion and an open ear for my troubles, and thank him for his soft tear-absorbent fur.

I believe that pets and people are predestined to meet each other on certain parts of their timeline to learn from and love one another. I came into Nitro's life when he was frightened and alone and gave him a home; he in return stayed with me through all the important life changes and became the stable portion of my life when everything else was changing rapidly.

Because of him I look at life differently. I try and find joy in the little things, like going for a walk, enjoying the sunshine, the comfort of a soft bed, and the happiness of finding wild catnip.

Seeking Help

Let me start by looking at a key question that I get asked regularly: 'When should someone seek face-to-face professional support when grieving?'

For some, professional help is needed immediately; others may need it after a period of time has passed, and yet others never need it at all. Only you (and possibly your doctor) know when and if you require some additional support. There is an exception to this, and that is if you are suffering from post-traumatic stress disorder (PTSD). If you are suffering with this often-overlooked condition, you do need professional medical help. All the books in the world won't help you navigate this clinical condition, so if you have any PTSD symptoms, please talk to your GP immediately. Symptoms of PTSD, in case you aren't familiar, may include flashbacks, nightmares and insomnia, difficulty focusing or concentrating, excessive worry about yourself or others, and a sense of feeling on high alert. The quicker you get help, the better and more effective treatment can be, so delaying treatment is detrimental. Once PTSD is being treated, you will be able to effectively process your grief.

If at any point you feel hopeless or suicidal, please seek professional help without delay. It is not weak to admit to needing help; in fact, it takes a special kind of strength.

This is my general checklist to gauge whether people need professional face-to-face support, and if you answer 'yes' to any of these questions I would encourage you to seek help (from a doctor, nurse, grief counsellor or clinical therapist):

* Do you feel stuck in grief and unable to move forwards?
* Do you feel the waves of grief are getting worse over time?
* Are you reliving the trauma on a regular basis?
* Are you feeling desperate?
* Do you feel vacant and removed from the world?
* Are you struggling to return to work?
* Are you unable to socialise or mix with friends or family (feeling this initially is normal, but after some time a person should be happy to re-engage with the outside world)?
* Are you avoiding things and feeling unable to face them?
* Are you struggling to eat or sleep?
* Are you relying on alcohol or other substances to help you survive?
* Are you suffering from panic attacks or anxiety that you are finding difficult or impossible to control?

Should I ask my doctor for medication?

I am not a GP and so won't even attempt to tackle this subject in my book. Some people need tablets to stabilise their emotions before grief can even start to be processed, while for others medication might actually prevent them from processing their grief. If you feel you need medication to help you (whether that be antidepressants or sleeping tablets), talk to your doctor. Your GP can and will help you.

Please also be aware that if you have any past history of depression or any other mental health conditions, grief can act as a trigger, so chat to your doctor as quickly as possible after suffering any form of bereavement.

'I have sometimes thought of the final cause of dogs having such short lives and I am quite satisfied it is in compassion to the human race; for if we suffer so much in losing a dog after an acquaintance of ten or twelve years, what would it be if they were to live double that time?'

Sir Walter Scott

Dek

The last question my mum asked me before I went under anaesthetic was, 'What do you want when you wake up?' My reply: 'A dog!' That was my earliest memory of Dek.

Dek was adopted at the age of five from Tameside Animal Shelter as a present after I went through life-saving brain surgery. Dek was an aid to me and helped me to walk again by giving me something to focus on. My recovery would have been a lot more difficult and delayed if it hadn't been for Dek.

He came with his issues: not cat-friendly, separation anxiety and toileting in the house. But then why would the 'perfect dog' be at a rehoming shelter?

He settled himself in very quickly by eating shoes, Xbox controllers, phones and remotes – he also loved to get into the bin given the chance. This behaviour quickly subsided and he started to bark instead!

Over the next few years we did everything to keep him happy and content: he would run and chase a tennis ball for hours on end, or he'd be happy to sit still next to you on the sofa and sleep for a full day!

Dek's personality grew and grew. He learned to love every single animal put in front of him, and was always there to lend a helping nose, ready to sniff any bum! Once I started working at a vet's he joined me every day, sleeping under the desk and sneaking out when he heard an animal crying in reception. Many times I looked over to the waiting area, did a double-take and said to myself, 'I recognise that dog!' He became a firm favourite with the clients and my colleagues. He would allow you to dress him in anything, and he LOVED being a little guinea pig for the student nurses learning how to bandage. One of the nurses went out of her way to bake him a cake on his 14th birthday, and he lapped up the attention.

He'd seen me grow up and I'd started to watch him grow older and slower. By now his poor legs affected him badly. He was on daily medication and we found out he had cruciate ligament damage. We had a decision to make in July 2016, whether to put him through surgery or not. After much thought, and knowing he still had a love for life, we went ahead with the operation.

His recovery went amazingly smoothly, he even received a bag full of treats and a 'get well soon' card from his work colleagues. He was like a new dog, and although he still had a minor limp, he would slyly run up and down the stairs and play with his beloved tennis ball as much as his little legs would let him.

In April 2017 we arranged a photoshoot for him on Lytham beach; we'd not been to the beach for around eight years so you can imagine just how happy and excited he was when his paws touched the sand. That whole day not once did he look like he was struggling on his legs, he loved every single minute of it. He ran after his ball, posed in every position possible, sat in bluebells, ran up the dunes and slept for a straight seven hours when we got home.

July 2017 quickly came around and we'd booked another photoshoot, this time with our cats, Rogue and Raven. Dek had to be carried to the studio due to his sore legs, but again he sat in front of the camera and owned it! Anything for food!

Upon returning home that evening, though, Dek's behaviour and mood changed, he started nonstop panting, his gums were white with a yellow tinge, and his stomach had started to swell at a rapid pace. Although we managed to settle him for the night, I was worried about the outcome of this.

The next day he came to work with me as normal and I asked for some bloods to be run on him. Within 24 hours I had the news I'd been dreading but expecting. I could opt for further investigations to find out why his stomach had swollen up or I could let him go with dignity.

My happy little boy had become a sad, depressed, unhappy little soul, and I knew what I needed to do. I had made a promise to Dek, that when the time came when he was no longer enjoying his life any more, I wouldn't be selfish and let him suffer, I would let him go with dignity.

During that week, friends, family, clients and colleagues all rallied round to come and say their goodbyes to him. The day before he was due to be put to sleep, we decided to take him back to the beach one last time. The poor little soul couldn't walk far, and we took it in turns between three of us to carry him around Lytham, then we walked right down into the water so his little feet could touch the water one last time.

One week after his final photoshoot, we all sat in the garden and waited for Dek's vet to come around. Dek sat in the sunshine as he'd always loved to do. When the time came, he lay down on his bed and passed his paw to his vet, I counted his final breaths, one, two, three . . . my boy was gone. I didn't feel sad instantly, I felt relief because he wasn't suffering any more. Dek stayed at home that night with us so we could spend just a little more time with him. We slept in the living room with him and wrapped him up in his favourite blankets. Raven never left his side.

In the months following the loss of Dek, I became very isolated and depressed; I suffered a breakdown and have since been on medication to cope with my anxiety and depression. Dek had given me a daily purpose to get up and focus my attention on someone. Without my daily dose of Dek I soon realised my happiness had gone. Although I had done what I selflessly had to do to ensure he left with dignity, I never considered my emotions following his death. As a pet owner, Dek's quality of life meant more to me than the unconditional love I had for him. I had to be selfless. You never get over the death of a loved one, you can only get through it. Grief is not a sign of weakness, nor a lack of faith, it is the price of love. Forever in my heart and my thoughts.

The Early Days After Loss

The early stages of loss are merciless, and to portray it as anything other than that would be unfair and untrue. The feelings are all-consuming and overpowering. They blindside you and can even make you want to die. It is scary and unsettling and nothing can prepare you for it, but knowing that it's 'normal' to feel these things helps, because when you are the one experiencing them you feel like you are going mad. So, let me reassure you, if you are feeling all these things right now, you aren't mad – you are heartbroken.

The initial days often go one of two ways. Some people switch to autopilot and just automatically do all the things that need to be done. They call people to inform them of the news, they make meals, they go through their check-list and carry out each task as if they are on a military assignment – this is the brain's way of surviving the initial trauma, and shock is helping them to carry on. It's a basic human response that most are born with, a fight-or-flight response to trauma: if someone is about to attack us, we run, we get to a place of safety before we allow our brains to process what has just happened.

Some people, on the other hand, shut down. They aren't even able to do basic tasks, as their brain has just pulled the plug and said, 'Nope, I just can't go there.' It's like an overheating computer shutting down automatically. This can happen just for a few hours, but for some it lasts a few days. If it's longer than a few days, I would always advise the person to seek professional help.

Once the initial shock dissipates, the 'missing them' kicks in. The void that they left in the world becomes a great big massive hole right in front of you, and you can do very little but stare at it. This is when the brain has realised your pet has gone forever and now has to come to terms with their absence. Even if you were expecting the loss and felt prepared for it, nothing can actually help your brain deal with this period of time.

I always say it is like a trapdoor has appeared and you suddenly fall. Life is okay one second, and totally changed the next. Every morning, after my own losses, I would wake up and be hit by a fresh new wave of grief. There was no escape – every time a wave went over my head, it was like hearing the news that they had died all over again. It felt like I had been run over by a huge truck in a hit-and-run accident, but the lorry just kept coming back and hitting me again and again. Each time it would fling me into the air, and I would pray that was the last time it would make contact, but no, it would find me wherever I hid and hit me from a different angle.

The next stage after losing a pet is often characterised by leaving you feeling out of control, and a natural reaction is to try to take back control of things as much as possible: doing household chores, for example, undertaking work projects, or any other activities which provide distraction.

It's the brain's way of trying to restore order. As it can't control the grief cycle and the feelings that can surface without warning, it encourages you to take control of other things. These tasks are probably completely unrelated to the loss, and at times such behaviour can seem highly irrational to those surrounding the bereaved person. If you have any leanings towards obsessive compulsive disorder (OCD), this stage can be magnified.

> 'Until one has loved an animal, a part of one's soul remains unawakened.'
>
> Anatole France

What to expect

Here are the emotional reactions that are widely recognised as being symptoms of grief:

* Shock
* Worry
* Anger
* Guilt
* Regret
* Confusion
* Relief
* Disbelief
* Denial
* Sadness
* Upset
* Acceptance

I am sure you can list even more. Grief is like a rollercoaster and a person can experience many different emotions and feelings over just a 30-minute period. This is what adds to that feeling of being out of control – you literally have no clue how you may feel from one minute to the next.

There are also many physical reactions, because grieving is a body, mind and spirit experience. Here are some common responses:

* Headaches
* Issues with sleeping – either too much or not enough
* Lack of appetite (or at times an increased appetite – comfort eating – depending on your relationship with food)
* Nausea
* Stomach cramps
* Upset stomach (diarrhoea or constipation)
* Lack of interest in sex or physical affection (or at times an increased desire depending on your relationship with sexual intimacy)
* Outbursts of anger or frustration
* Restless legs or numbness
* Racing heart or feelings of panic
* Nightmares
* Teeth or jaw issues (due to grinding your teeth or clenching your jaw)
* Depression (which is different from grieving)
* Low immunity (which can mean you catch more colds and viruses)

If you are concerned about any of the symptoms you are experiencing, please consult your doctor. While many physical symptoms can be linked to grief, it is very important to make sure there aren't other underlying medical conditions that are being overlooked, so please don't just assume that anything you are experiencing is connected to your loss; visit your doctor to be on the safe side.

What is normal?

Often people worry about what is normal, so let me reassure you that the following are common when grieving:

* Lacking motivation
* Feeling tired
* Inability to concentrate
* Inability to make decisions (sometimes even the most basic everyday ones)
* Inability to remember even basic information and facts
* Feeling lost and like you aren't in your own body
* Lack of identity and struggling to remember who you are
* Being unhappy or unsettled in your job (and questioning your career path)
* Uncertainty about key relationships and questioning how happy/satisfied you are with them
* Feeling insecure about things you need to do
* Being unstable emotionally
* Craving to be alone
* Conversely, craving to be with people and not alone (possibly being scared of being alone)
* Fearing the future
* Feeling impatient and having a much lower anger or irritation threshold

* Being intolerant of things that never previously bothered you
* Feeling the world is unjust and unfair
* Being fearful of carrying out normal tasks
* Being fearful of death or losing other loved ones
* Fearing something going wrong with yourself physically or mentally
* Having a desire to pack up and travel the world

'His ears were often the first thing to catch my tears.'

Elizabeth Barrett Browning

Max

When I was a student at New York University, my dorm was across the street from Washington Square Park. I loved going to the dog run and watching the different breeds of dogs playing together. My favourite of all the breeds was the Pembroke Welsh Corgi. These red and white foxlike dogs seemed to always be having fun. They brightened my days with their big ears and adorable tailless back ends. They were so fast and playful. I told myself one day I would have one.

After college, I moved back home and it was difficult to find a job in my industry. I had studied Music Business, there were only a small number of companies in New York and everyone wanted in. I decided since I was working at a local book store and had free time I would look for a corgi of my own. I found a breeder several hours away, but the trip to get my puppy was well worth it.

I brought home my first baby during a snowstorm. I will never forget that day. My boy's parents were show dogs and since he had champion blood in him I gave him a fancy name: Maximilian Winter Romance, Max for short. He was only 10 weeks old when he came to live with me. We had a Westie named Scotty at home that was our family dog and he was 10 years old. Max was the first dog that was truly mine. He was adorable, fluffy, fun and so incredibly smart.

Scotty soon warmed to Max because no one could resist him. They spent many hours together cuddling.

Max quickly became my best friend. He made us laugh by taking his food into another room and tossing it in the air before eating it. He ran around the house each night after dinner. As a puppy and herding dog, he believed my sister Pam was something he should herd! I loved training and playing with Max; he loved it too. We would play hide-and-seek and it was amazing how good he was at it. He could find any toy or person I told him to. Up and down the stairs, in and out of every room. I could leave a treat in front of Max on the floor and leave the room. Max wouldn't touch it until I said it was okay. He never drank water and instead would sit by the fridge and bark twice when he wanted an ice cube. He was such a character!

Max was there for me through the years for all the best and worst times in life. His bright eyes seemed to speak volumes when I needed it most. My sister was diagnosed with brain cancer and right after her operation I too had to have surgery to remove a benign mass. It was such a scary time in my life and Max was right by my side. When I finally landed a job in the music business, Max was there to celebrate by jumping around with excitement. It didn't matter what I was joyful about, Max was always excited for me!

When I got married, Max was right there with me in the pictures wearing a bow tie with a smile on his face. He was so loved that when my husband and I moved into our apartment my parents asked to have him for sleepovers. When I would walk Max in our new neighbourhood and he lost his sense of where he was, he would just stop walking. He would stand still and refuse to budge. I did the only thing I could for my best friend and carried him home.

Shortly after my niece was born, Pam's brain cancer returned with a vengeance. She passed away aged 33, only 11 months after her daughter Casey was born. It was the absolute worst time of my life, but Max was there. He sat on my lap when I cried, licked away my tears and even helped watch over my niece. Max was always there to support me and he meant the world to me.

At only six years old Max became critically ill and we couldn't figure out what was wrong. I remember praying for him to recover and thinking I wouldn't know what to do without him. The emergency vet asked if I wanted to spend the money needed to save him. I had never been so offended. I would have spent every penny on my Max. After multiple blood transfusions and medication, they were able to stabilise him, then our personal vet cared for him and ultimately saved his life. Max was diagnosed with an autoimmune disease called Evan's syndrome. From that point on he saw our vet regularly and was on lifetime medication. We had a couple of scares, but thankfully he always pulled through. He became a favourite at the vet, which was no surprise to me. Max later developed another condition that prevented him from using his back legs, but he never lost his spirit.

Just before Max's 14th birthday he developed seizures. The vet suspected a brain tumour, but at his age testing and treatment wasn't an option. So on 23 November 2011, I had to say goodbye to my best friend and first baby. I held him as he took his last breath and, although it was painful for me, I knew he needed me there to help him cross the rainbow bridge. I couldn't leave him alone at the end because he never left me alone in life.

When Max passed I was devastated. Losing him left a huge hole in my heart. I couldn't believe that I had lost my Max to a brain tumour, just as I had lost Pam years earlier. At times it was unbearable, but through my grief I learned two important lessons. The first was that I was blessed to have had Max in my life for almost 14 years. I missed him so very much, but he would always be in my heart and thoughts. The second was that I owed it to him and my sister to live life to the fullest. Max was smart, happy and left an imprint on everyone he met. I wanted to appreciate all of my life in his honour.

It has been many years since my Max passed. I have lost many people in my life since and each loss has changed me. I have never and will never stop loving or missing my Max. People who have never had a pet cannot understand the love and bond between pet and parent. In many ways Max was my first baby. He taught me how to care for others. He taught me patience, understanding and unconditional love. If I hadn't been blessed with Max I would have missed out on so much and my life would never have felt complete.

When Will the Grief and the 'Missing Them' Feelings End?

I know only too well why people want to know this. I would have paid big money to find out the answer myself, but as grief is unique to every single person, there is no set answer. While this can be incredibly frustrating and also scary (as we all want to know the rollercoaster will end sometime soon), it can also be encouraging.

This might seem counter-intuitive, but we all know people who are stuck in grief and have never moved forwards. When we are going through grief ourselves, we look at these people in terror, thinking that this is how we will also now be forever. But I can confidently say to you today, that's not how it will be if you don't want it to be – that is *their* walk through grief, not yours. You control your walk and you can heal; you can come out of the dark part of grief, and I hope this book will show you that.

What might help is to forget many of the myths you may have been taught or told about grief – for example, that the worst part of grief is the first week – because many of the clichés that people come out with about grief are just that. The false expectation that we put on ourselves, or that others have put on us, becomes the block over which we stumble, so remove it – throw it away. You will grieve for as long as you need to grieve and not a day less than that!

As far as missing your pet is concerned, to be honest, I don't think it ever ends, but in my own experience it did become easier to live with. Once the shock had passed and life became 'normal' again, those feelings just sat comfortably alongside everyday life, and I built my life around that hole, a hole that can never be filled in. I think you adjust to it, as you don't want it to disappear. Death made that hole appear, but love actually created it. It was only because you loved your pet that the hole made by their loss is so big and so deep, and so meaningful.

Grief is hard work, but if you can understand the process it is less overwhelming. By learning about the patterns and associated symptoms, you can reach a point where you feel as if you are controlling it, rather than the other way around. You are able to pre-empt potential waves and, when they do hit, you can be somewhat prepared. For instance, if you know that every morning at the time when you would normally take your pet for a walk the grief consumes you, set that time aside each day and create a new daily ritual. Perhaps this is the time each day you take out a journal and write down how you feel?

I would encourage you to be an active participant in processing your grief, and not just become a sitting duck. The more you consciously face the pain and the trauma of loss and grief, the quicker you will emerge from the blackest part of the grieving process. It is not going to be easy, or pretty – in fact, it could be the hardest battle of your life, and a billion tears may need to be shed – but you will survive it.

'There is a sacredness in tears. They are not the mark of weakness, but of power. They speak more eloquently than ten thousand tongues. They are the messengers of overwhelming grief, of deep contrition, and of unspeakable love.'

Washington Irving

Suzie

Ever since I was little I've had a strong love of animals. The one pet I'd always wanted was a dog. Every Christmas it was at the top of my list but I was always told no. I had other pets growing up – hamsters, rabbits and guinea pigs, etc. – but never a dog.

In 2004 at 21 years old I decided to buy my first house with my then boyfriend. The following year we saw an advert for Shih Tzu puppies and I was so excited. We spent some time with the owners and the litter and eventually chose a gorgeous champagne and white little girl. She was so tiny and a complete living, breathing teddy bear. Driving home, we were talking names and I remembered I had a champagne-coloured cuddly toy dog that my grandparents gave me as a baby which was called Suzie. That became the name of my gorgeous new little puppy.

Suzie settled in so well and became the centre of my attention. We'd spend weekends walking in the park and away on camping trips; basically, any time I wasn't at work we would be together. The following year we heard Suzie's parents were having another litter and this time her brother joined our family – we called him Archie. From then on both of them would spend every evening sitting on me like proper lapdogs.

Then in 2006 my world started to crumble. Up until this point I had never experienced upset or grief; I guess that's lucky for someone in their twenties. One night I received the news my grandad had terminal cancer. I went home and sobbed on the sofa, and this was the point that Suzie jumped up and nuzzled into me to comfort me. I knew she knew I was upset. The following weeks were difficult as my grandad went downhill quickly and passed away four weeks after diagnosis. Throughout all the tears, Suzie was the one who comforted me and was always there.

Later that year we moved to a larger, more expensive house with a lovely big back garden for the dogs to play in.

In 2007 I went off to university to study dental hygiene and therapy. It was an intense and very stressful course and I commuted to another city as well. During my time at uni, my long-term boyfriend and I got married, one of my best friends died in a car accident, I suffered with psoriasis which caused alopecia and my husband lost his job (which was supporting us while I studied). Throughout it all Suzie was there every night without fail, sitting on my knee, nuzzling me and comforting me.

Things at home began to get worse. My husband found temporary jobs but hated them and would come home in an awful mood and I would dread hearing his key turn in the door. Finally, in 2013 as I turned 30 years old we separated and divorced. I moved back in with my parents, bringing Suzie and Archie with me of course. There was no way I was going to give them up even though it was suggested I rehome them so I could rent. There was no way I was going to do that.

Eventually I met a new guy and in 2014 we moved in together. Obviously, my little Suzie and her brother moved in too.

Two years later saw the unexpected loss of my grandma. We were extremely close and I was devastated. For months and months, I cried every night with Suzie by my side or on my knee. She used to come with me to visit Grandma's grave as well. The first few times I took her she would sniff around the grave and whimper.

One evening it was raining outside and I was home alone with the dogs. I came in from doing something in the back garden and slipped on the kitchen floor. I went down heavily and lay there for ages not daring to move, as I was sure I'd broken something. As I was lying there Archie walked past me and went to his food bowl for some supper. I was confused at this point as to where Suzie was. I managed to look round and realised she was sitting right by the top of my head looking down at me, and she didn't move until I managed to get up and give her a hug. Luckily, I was just bruised and nothing was broken.

In April 2017 my partner and I decided to try for a baby and couldn't believe it when in June that year we found out I was pregnant. However, a few weeks later I started bleeding and getting one-sided pain. Hospital scans showed our baby was ectopic and I was given the methotrexate injection to stop the pregnancy. The experience and loss were horrific and I felt so lonely. Suzie was my only comfort. I recovered, however, and we decided to try again. On New Year's Eve we got our second positive test, but this was short-lived as I miscarried by mid-January. I fell pregnant twice more that year, with the same unhappy results. While all this was going on, Suzie once again was by my side the whole time providing love and support.

In 2019 Suzie turned 14 years old. I could see her health starting to deteriorate. She had the occasional fit and completely lost her sight. But whenever I would get home from work and say, 'Hey, baby girl', Suzie would still wiggle with excitement and wag her tail. Throughout the year she got worse, though; she would pace about and not know where she was.

On the evening of 9 December 2019 Suzie passed away while we were cuddling on the sofa watching TV. My beautiful girl, who had been through everything with me, was gone. To this day I still struggle with her loss and as I write this now there are tears.

Since losing Suzie we have lost three more babies between 2020 and 2021, and we are about to embark on our IVF journey. Suzie's little brother Archie is now over 15 years old and is showing early signs of doggy dementia too. I miss Suzie with all my heart and always wish she was here to comfort me through my pregnancy losses. She really was my world.

Issues Around Euthanasia

What does the word 'euthanasia' mean? It means the act or practice of ending the life of something or someone who is very sick or injured in order to prevent any more suffering.

The decision to euthanise a pet who is very sick is the most beautiful gift and selfless act of love one could ever give. You are suffering so your beloved animal doesn't need to. All that being said, it doesn't mean you won't feel guilty about the decision, or even question if you made the right judgement call. The fact that you are having to process all your feelings about your decision at a time of great grief magnifies those feelings of doubt and guilt. It can take some time before you are able to rationally and calmly know and accept that you did the very best thing for your companion.

In terms of pet ownership, there are not many more distressing tasks than considering euthanising a pet, or having to actually watch your pet take its last breath. I don't think anything in life can prepare you for those moments. I have been in the room four times witnessing our dogs pass over the rainbow bridge. Each time was horrific and, if I'm honest, I think I left a little part of myself in those rooms. I somehow managed to hold myself together every time while the injections were administered. I felt it was my final gift to our dogs to be as calm as I could muster, and I wanted them to feel peace in their last minutes on earth. I lay on the floor with them, or rested my head on theirs on the table and told them that everything was going to be okay. I whispered in their ears how much I loved them, and as they slipped away I stroked their heads.

I want to talk about the moments that followed their passing . . . as that's when my world changed every time.

I didn't need to hold it together any more; they had left the room and the black veil of grief fell instantly. It sounds dramatic to say I could hardly breathe in the hours that followed their deaths, but it's true. I felt like my chest was caving in and the pain was real.

To enter the vet's with your beloved pet and to leave with empty arms is a massive shock to the system. I am sure every one of you has a heartbreaking story to tell, and part of all our healing comes from telling those stories. Our brains can be easily traumatised and, when it comes to losing anyone or anything you love, there is trauma at the heart of the loss. So please find someone you can trust to share your story with; you may need to tell it over and over again before you can (reluctantly) accept what has happened.

As you enter those first few hours of grief you may feel numb, in shock, or utterly consumed – there is no right or wrong way to feel. You may have been told that grief had neat stepping stones, 'the seven stages', a sequential pattern that could be formally danced, like an agonising waltz. But it's simply not true – grieving is messy and illogical. Every bereaved person has their own personal steps to take and an individual path to navigate. This is why grief is as unique as one's fingerprints, so take it a day at a time; and, if that's too long, an hour at a time.

Grief has many agonising layers to it, perhaps one of the worst being the terrifying reality that we have no power to control who stays and who leaves this planet. This realisation can make many bereaved people feel utterly out of control, and a common response is to start fearing other animals or people we love may also pass away. If you are experiencing this, please know this is a stage of grief and often these feelings and worries settle over time. If the fear increases, however, or doesn't leave, talking with a counsellor or therapist can really help.

Nebu

Making the decision to say goodbye to my horse, Nebu, was without a doubt the hardest decision I have ever made and one that I am not sure I will ever come to terms with.

I was not born into a 'horsey' family but caught the equine bug pretty early on in life, always feeling that being around horses brought me a sense of peace that nothing else could. I was never the most confident rider and mostly just enjoyed being in the presence of horses, feeling their warm breath on my skin and watching them graze.

I'd always dreamed of having my own horse – it was on every Christmas list as a child and I even used to sometimes dream I was adopted, and my real family owned a ranch in Montana and would one day bring me to live with them where I could ride horses in the mountains every day – but it took me almost 30 years before I finally achieved my dream of owning a horse. I had recently come out of a difficult relationship, lost my home and was plagued by depression. I'd moved home to live with my mother, was struggling at work and really didn't see the point in life any more. To put it bluntly, I needed a reason to live, and that reason turned out to be a 10-year-old thoroughbred ex-racehorse. His name was Nebu and he had the gentlest eyes, with a coat the colour of liquid gold. He had recently retired from a long career in flat racing after a tendon injury and had subsequently been passed around several unsuitable and neglectful homes before being sold as 'perfect for a novice' – and so, naive and infatuated, I bought him.

I realised very quickly that I was completely out of my depth; luckily, a lady at the stables where I kept him took me under her wing and taught me how to care for him. We had a few weeks of relaxing countryside rides and 'living the dream' before things went rapidly downhill. Nebu started to become spooky at the slightest thing, and began bucking when saddled, resulting in me having three falls in the space of a week. I was left wondering what on earth I had taken on. Everyone around me told me to sell him or put him down. The vet who saw him said he was psychologically damaged from racing, the farrier said he was beyond help, the equine dentist said he had the worst teeth he had ever seen, and the riding instructor said to give up on him before he killed me.

I didn't give up. I did give up trying to ride him, but I poured all my energy into learning everything I could about why he might be behaving nervously. I started building our relationship again, from the ground up, getting to know each other, with no pressure on him to do anything that he didn't want to. I treated his stomach, where he was riddled with painful gastric ulcers, overhauled his nutrition, found a farrier, instructor, physiotherapist, dentist and vet who believed they could help him, and I assured Nebu that he was safe now. I didn't do everything right, I didn't do every test under the sun, and I didn't give up hope of riding him again, but I tried to be open-minded to different ways to help him and to give him time, something he had never really been afforded.

We had a rollercoaster few years together – one week we would be trotting across stubble fields and he would be following me around like a puppy, the next week he would be rearing up above me as a I tried to lead him and he would look thoroughly miserable and be dropping weight by the day. I so badly wanted to give him the gift of a peaceful retirement and for him to know what it was to be loved and safe after such a traumatic life. I so badly wanted to save him. But in November 2017, I decided that he'd had enough. His behaviour was increasingly unpredictable, and I know that it was because he was in pain – even though he was retired, he wasn't happy or healthy. After years of battling to improve his health, when I finally made the decision to have him euthanised there was a part of me that anticipated an element of relief afterwards.

But I was wrong. From the moment the lethal injection went in, Nebu dropped to the ground and I held him in my arms as he took his last breath, I felt nothing but indescribable, all-consuming grief.

I also felt guilt, betrayal and confusion, knowing that I was the one responsible for ending his life. Despite the experience being quick, humane and peaceful, I fear that I will always be plagued by crippling 'what-ifs'. The what-ifs are worsened, not alleviated as I'd hoped, by the fact that I went on to sign up to a master's degree course in equine behaviour. What if I'd known then what I now? What if he wasn't telling me that he'd had enough, and was instead telling me not to give up? What if I'd made a mistake and we weren't at the end of the road, I just needed to have tried one more thing and it would be the magical cure? I felt like

I'd given up on him when I'd promised him that I would never do that.

When the decision is not clear cut and straightforward, it's hard not to second-guess yourself, let alone if you have a multitude of people around you all offering their opinion. But I try to remind myself that, at the time, I genuinely believed that he was telling me to let him go; and sometimes in life, there are worse things than death. If I had sold Nebu on when people around me first told me to, he might have faced a far more traumatic outcome than a peaceful and humane death.

Would I rather have said that goodbye a moment too soon, or prolonged his suffering by saying it a moment too late? Should I have kept him here with me, selfishly and desperately, because I couldn't imagine life without him and couldn't bear to let him go? Or should I have set him free from pain and distress, even if it meant that I would take on that pain and distress myself in my grief? Some people say that you know when it's time. I'm not sure that's true, because the fact is that you can't make an objective assessment when so many emotions are involved. However, we owe it to our incredible, selfless, sentient animal companions to give them not only a good life experience but also the gift of a good farewell.

Several years after losing Nebu, I have almost learned to live with the ache that remains, in the knowledge that he is at peace and my grief is part of who I am now. Today, I work in equine welfare and am studying for a PhD investigating equine welfare at end-of-life, specifically looking at those horses who aren't guaranteed a humane death and get sent to slaughter. Many of these come from the racing industry and, unlike Nebu, don't get given a second chance at life. It is Nebu – my golden boy – who first guided me down this path that I continue to explore and so it's a comfort to know that he did not die in vain. He lives on, in all the work I do for equine welfare, and in every breath I take, because I am a dreamer, and he was my dream.

The Shame Connected to Pet Loss Grief

I don't know about you, but this was a big issue for me. I even felt embarrassed to say I was grieving for my pet, for fear of ridicule. This is important, because if people are made to feel silly for grieving it can make a person hide their pain and lock away their grief, neither of which is healthy or productive.

Grief and loss are often ranked by society – i.e. 'x loss is worse than y loss' – and I long to see this changed. As a grief specialist, I know that pain is relative to each person's journey: what affects one person majorly may have little impact on another. Loss can also compound other issues, so a seemingly small, inconsequential loss can be a trigger for some, and it may reveal deep-rooted pain and trauma from the past. The bottom line is that no one should evaluate or judge other people's grief and pain – let the grieving person tell you why and how much it hurts and don't presume anything.

Things people who lose a pet often hear that can induce shame:

* 'How can this upset you so much when you have been through so much in the past?'
* 'They were just a pet, at least you didn't lose a person you love.'
* 'X lost y, which was so much worse than your loss.'
* 'Why don't you just get another pet?'
* 'Just do something to take your mind off the pain.'
* 'You need to distract yourself.'
* 'You should just be grateful you had your pet for so long.'
* 'Losing a pet is nothing like losing a person though, is it?'
* 'My friend lost their pet and they were only upset for a week.'
* 'You must be relieved they are out of pain.'
* 'I am sure you will feel better next week.'
* 'As soon as you get another pet the pain will go.'
* 'I think you should put this pain into perspective.'

Although often said with good intentions, any phrase or line that minimises someone's experience can bring shame and hurt, so it is imperative that words are carefully selected.

'Everyone can master a grief but he that has it.'

William Shakespeare

Scrappy

I had my boxer dog Scrappy put to sleep on 19 March 2021 when he was 10 years old. I have three other dogs including his brother.

I love all four of my dogs, but Scrappy was my soul dog, my shadow, my rock and my protector. If anything felt wrong, he was there guarding me; he knew his mum was struggling a lot mentally. He was the family protector, and if any of my other dogs disappeared, he would round them up. He was a clown, so funny and entertaining; his nickname was Artful Dodger, a little angel disguised as a devil.

January 2020 saw the break-up of my unhappy and unpleasant relationship. My dogs helped me through it all, and they've seen and heard things nobody else will ever know. When I was living on my own for the first time, Scrappy was my constant comfort and in telling me, 'It's okay, Mum, I'm here,' that dog was my life support. I wanted so badly to give up many times, but I knew I couldn't leave my dogs and I knew Scrappy would never cope without his mum. I can honestly say without my dogs I wouldn't be here now.

During Covid, with a stalking case and other problems going on I really struggled, and my anxiety was worse than ever. But my dogs gave me the strength and courage to fight, because I had to make sure we had a roof over our heads. Sadly, Scrappy can't be here to see I made it through, but I know he'd be proud of me.

I first noticed Scrappy was drinking/urinating excessively around September 2020. He collapsed one weekend, so we went straight to the vet's. I had this gut instinct something serious was wrong. He went through many tests and scans until they eventually diagnosed pancreatitis. He was given medication and a special diet but Scrappy deteriorated and was hospitalised for two nights. He came home and was eating again, but he'd lost a lot of weight. The battle went on and he needed a lot of care.

I tried him with everything I could think of – even venison burgers! – but he was still losing weight and spent three more nights at the vet's. I fought so hard and tried everything imaginable. It broke me many times, as just when I thought we were starting to break through he'd go back downhill. I spent a lot of time sitting on my kitchen floor screaming and crying for him to just get better. It was an emotional rollercoaster; I'd have given anything to make him better.

In his last few weeks, he had lost so much weight and was getting very weak, but I still couldn't make that final decision. So many things in my head: 'How can I end my dog's life?'; 'What if he can get better?'; 'How do you know it's time?' Then one Monday morning, I cooked him his venison and he turned away. I knew there and then he'd never eat again. I saw it in him, he'd given up, he looked at me as if to say, 'Mum, I'm done.' That broke me, my whole world felt like it was over. I couldn't talk about it without crying my eyes out.

A friend rang the vet's for me to ask about the process of euthanasia during the pandemic. They said that due to Covid restrictions I couldn't accompany him, they had to take him in first to prepare him. I thought, *That's not how my boy is going, we are not being separated and I will be with him all the way.* So I found a lovely vet who agreed to do it at my home and booked it in.

The feeling of knowing what I had arranged made me physically sick. I didn't even know how to cope with having booked my dog's death. To me he was like my child. Imagine booking in a child's death? However, I knew I couldn't leave him to suffer in pain or starve to death.

For the last two nights before the agreed day, I lay on the sofa with him all night. We'd never spent a night apart; I've always had my dogs on my bed. We cuddled so much those nights, exactly how he loved to spend his time. Always touching his mum! He was the cuddliest dog I've ever known. I stroked his head constantly and I told him how much I loved him.

On the day, one of my friends was there with me and my other three dogs were all present. The vet was lovely but professional. The dread of it all makes you so sick and the waiting was awful. Taking him outside into the garden for the last time was probably the worst thing that sticks in my mind!

During it I held him all the way through, stroking him, cuddling him, telling him he was the best dog in the world. I told him not to worry about me, and I promised to look after his brother for him. The one thing I'll always take away from it is that it was the most peaceful passing I've ever seen. There wasn't a dramatic last breath, he just peacefully slipped away in my arms.

Then the grief began. I've never felt pain like it in my life. And, my word, it comes in waves that can knock you off your feet. At one point I just collapsed in a heap on the floor and could not move for a long time. Nothing can prepare you for it, I couldn't sit on his sofa for days. The grief was beyond belief, I was absolutely broken not having him there. I couldn't eat, focus or function.

The first wave for me was just pure heartbreak and constant sadness. Then the waves came with guilt and 'what-ifs' soon after. I couldn't stomach it for the first week or so, I couldn't stomach that I'd killed my boy. That's how I saw it, and I couldn't deal with it. I felt like his brother hated me because he knew I'd killed Scrappy.

Now, though, I can and will say that your gut instinct knows. The vet who put him to sleep said there was undoubtedly cancer somewhere and I'd made the right decision, and that helped me feel some peace about it. The guilt I still feel now is that I wish I'd spent more time making his last weeks amazing, rather than fighting so hard to try and make him better.

One part of grief that I found hard was when I looked at my other dogs and all I could think was, 'You aren't Scrappy.' I love my other dogs but my bond with him was on another level. I felt awful for feeling like that when they were grieving too, especially his brother. They hadn't been separated since birth. And his brother was hitting my emotions hard, seeing him sad yet struggling to get myself together. But as Scrappy slipped away I promised him I would look after his brother and give him his best life, so I will honour that. There isn't a day goes by without me thinking about him and I still cry a lot over him.

I struggled to take my other dogs out for nice walks, it felt like now Scrappy was gone we could go out to nice places. (Scrappy couldn't really go on walks during the last few weeks.) But I remembered my promise to Scrappy and I knew he would want nothing more than for me and his siblings to get out and enjoy our time.

From this experience I've come to terms with the fact that there are worse fates than death. I've always seen death as the worst scenario or ending. But what would have been worse was watching my boy starve, or struggle to get up day after day or watching him throw up time and time again. Watching him on his last night being offered anything he wanted and him looking at it like he wished he could eat it but just couldn't hit hard. It doesn't mean death is easy, just that sometimes it is perhaps kinder.

As heartbroken as I am, I know I tried to do the absolute best for my boy. I may not have got it all right, but I tried my hardest for him. It took a massive toll on me, but I'd do it all again in a heartbeat.

For now, I get by knowing he's here with me in spirit until we meet again one day.

I've had a rocky 18 months, and my dogs have got me through every part. Things are slowly looking a little more positive now. I wish more than anything that Scrappy could have been here to enjoy the nicer times.

I will always be eternally grateful to my soul dog, my soldier, my hero, my baby, for getting me through the dark times I never believed I'd survive. He'll always have my whole heart and he took a big chunk of it with him when he went.

Layers of Grief

You may have read many articles and leaflets on grief and loss that assert that there are five set stages. These are usually:

* Denial
* Anger
* Bargaining
* Depression
* Acceptance

Some lists throw in shock and guilt for good luck and say there are seven stages. But while these lists can be accurate for some, those who go through grief via these steps, in this set order, will definitely be in the minority. Grief is not that straightforward.

It may be easier to talk about myself when explaining this. When our dog Jake died, I didn't go into denial. I never felt any anger about his death – either at myself or the vet – none, no anger at all. I didn't bargain. However, I did reach acceptance. I would say my stages of grief looked more like this:

* Shock
* Fear
* Shock (again)
* Loss
* Depression
* Acceptance

Each person's steps will be unique to them, even if there are strong common themes or similarities with those of others.

Grief really can come off in layers – one minute you can be fine and the next you are crying, and this can happen over weeks and months or even over a lifetime. It seems to be a commonly held belief that grief should have a time limit – it's fine to grieve for a certain period, then you should 'get over it'. And that acceptable time period is a lot shorter for the loss of a pet than of a person. The sad part of this is that it means most people continue to grieve in silence. This is especially true if a person didn't feel able to process their grief at the time of their loss. If years later they allow themselves time to process the pain, their acquaintances and colleagues often don't respect and acknowledge how vital this is to a person's well-being, and can make them feel shame for expressing their pain and sadness so long after the loss has happened.

Grief is a long journey; it will be patient and travel with a person until they are ready or able to process it.

One extra thing to realise is this: once you have survived a loss you are forever changed. I believe one of the ramifications of this is that, if you lose other pets or people you love in the future, you will never again grieve only for the animal or person who has just died, you will recommence grieving for all the ones you have loved and lost. This can make future losses more challenging, and you may quickly feel consumed with grief. Please try not to be scared: simply allow yourself to face the pain, and deal with the many grief layers that are being internally processed.

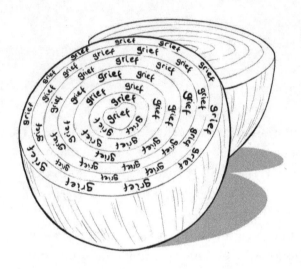

Buddie

Buddie was our handsome little Lakeland Terrier. He entered into our hearts and lives in 2011, when we adopted him from the SSPCA (the Scottish equivalent of the RSPCA). He was found wandering the streets of Glasgow, all alone and frightened.

Buddie was such a vulnerable little fella, all insecure and anxious. It became very apparent, quite quickly, that he had been mistreated in his first few months of life. His tail had been docked, and he was also exhausted and very withdrawn for the first few weeks living with me and my husband.

Graeme and I had married the previous year; I was 38 and Graeme a little older. Although we wanted our own family, unfortunately this never happened for us. We decided we would adopt a dog, and for me my maternal instinct and love was poured into this scared and vulnerable but beautiful dog that had become family very quickly.

Buddie became more confident around the home, with family and friends; he loved nothing more than to snuggle beside people he trusted on the sofa. He continued to be anxious and frightened outside, especially around other animals. Even after sessions with a behaviourist, he never fully gained trust around other owners and their dogs. We would keep him at a distance to help manage his fear.

Buddie was very much our 'wee boy' whom we loved and adored. My relationship with him was so close, especially as I started to experience health issues. Buddie was very intuitive to my feelings and would cuddle in tighter on the days I felt particularly unwell.

My health deteriorated over the next couple of years and in 2014, I was diagnosed with a progressive neuromuscular mitochondrial disease, which forced me to give up my career as a paediatric nurse and relinquish my nursing registration. Now at home full time with Buddie, our bond grew deeper and stronger. He would listen to all my hopes and dreams for a cure and, at times, all my worries and fears. His big brown eyes were so full of understanding.

As mitochondrial disease is genetic and is passed down from mother to child, I quietly resolved in my heart and mind that not having our own babies had actually been a blessing in disguise. My husband and I never made much of an issue or spoke much about it – we quietly accepted it was 'just meant to be'. I became more grateful and thankful for my little companion Buddie, on whom I could pour out all my maternal love and care.

Buddie came on holidays with us and we would book quiet rural holidays, so he would feel happy and secure. Places we could relax with him, knowing he would not need to have much interaction with other dogs, places he could run free on a beach or in a quiet woodland with no perceived threat. We adapted our garden and lifestyle to an extent, to make sure our sweet boy felt secure and happy.

Buddie definitely helped protect me from loneliness and isolation after giving up my nursing career. He was vulnerable and needed caring for in every way. My focus on Buddie gave me purpose and kept me from becoming self-absorbed or depressed at my situation.

In 2018 I noticed Buddie becoming clingier and more protective of me. Within a few weeks of this happening, I was diagnosed with breast cancer. This was such a shock and blow to myself, my husband and family. I was thrown into a world of countless hospital appointments, surgery, chemotherapy, radiotherapy and challenging discussions with oncologists. Once again Buddie was my little confidant at all times; he was always waiting behind the door with a wagging tail when I returned home from hospital. He was the one with whom I would share all my fears and worries, the ones you just don't want to burden your human family with. Buddie always listened and always cuddled in that little bit closer, especially when my husband was at work. He helped me through almost two years of treatment. He was my constant companion again, through the most difficult dark days.

He was also there through the good days, the days when I would receive good news, and in particular the words, 'You are cancer free, Mrs Scott,' Buddie was cuddled so tightly, with every emotion that poured out of me that particular day.

In 2020, during the Covid pandemic, Buddie had been suffering with recurrent infections that his vet was finding difficult to get on top of. He was on so many courses of antibiotics. His pain was affecting his behaviour, which in turn caused his fears and anxieties to become more intense. Buddie's comfort, routines and life were being challenged, beyond what he could cope with. After a couple of incidents while out on walks, mixed with the continued pain of his infections, Graeme and I had to have the difficult discussion of what was now best for Buddie, firstly between ourselves and then with the vet. Even after all I had faced with my own health, this was the most distressing conversation I had ever had.

It was decided on 15 June 2020 that Buddie would be put to sleep for his own comfort and welfare.

The instant grief we felt was all-consuming, it hit us both with such violent force. We were inconsolable. So many thoughts of guilt, questioning and helplessness came all at once. Buddie, for the first time in a long time, looked so content as he lay on the table, peaceful in his 'eternal sleep', yet Graeme and I were thrown into such a deep sense of loss and sadness. When we returned home the house felt so empty. Buddie's bed, toys and blankets were still there. His little pieces of fur were still stuck to the sofa, his blanket still smelled of him, yet Buddie had gone forever.

The first night was just awful. My whole belief system had been rocked in a few hours. I was questioning everything. Both Graeme and I are people of faith and live by our Christian values. I was overwhelmed by the most awful thought that I may never see Buddie again. Do dogs get into Heaven? Why would a loving God not let dogs into Heaven? Have I just gone against all I believe about euthanasia? My core values had just been challenged, mixed in with the deepest sense of loss and grief. I would previously often say that Buddie received the love that I had in my heart for the babies I had wanted. I'd always wanted three children and Buddie received all that love rolled into one. The pain of loss was so intense that first night.

The loss of Buddie brought to the surface the grief for other things I had suppressed over the years. My loss of motherhood, the loss of my career, the loss of my health. It took me a while to work through this and accept that I had a journey of healing to go on for many losses.

Ultimately, this was Buddie's lasting gift to me. Our love and bond were so deep, it took the love of Buddie to help me become a more whole, self-aware and healed person.

I miss my Buddie every day, yet I am so thankful that he came and rescued me, through those difficult times, especially as I initially thought it was us rescuing him. I am now content in the thought that having Buddie in our lives here on earth was enough. If he is just in an eternal sleep now, that is enough, as he is no longer suffering. If I do get to see him in Heaven, then oh, what a bonus that will be.

Buddie can never be replaced because our bond was so strong and unique. Yet our hearts are big and strong enough now to share that love with our little pug puppy, Jinty Joy. Jinty loves other dogs and is waiting for a little 'rescue' brother, who will be arriving into our hearts and home any day now. Our adventure continues.

Our hearts are forever grateful and thankful for our darling Buddie boy.

When Fear Is Controlling Your Joy

As my dog Jake got older I noticed how much the fear of losing him robbed me of the joy I once had taking care of him. This is perhaps one of the issues of loving a dog or a cat or many other animals: you are acutely aware that it's highly likely that you will outlive this pet sitting before you. You are painfully conscious that each year may be their last, and there aren't many other relationships that have this ticking clock being forever present.

I don't know exactly when I became consumed with the dread of Jake dying, but I assume it was after his first major stroke. In the following hours and weeks his mortality became a major obstacle to my peace.

As Jake changed from a young dog into a visibly elderly dog every illness he encountered filled me with dread. The earlier confidence that all would be well when we took him to the vet's was replaced by a certainty that his life was now limited and each month could be his last. As he aged he became more dependent on us, and where once we were happy to travel and leave family members to look after him, now his health meant we didn't want to leave others with this acute responsibility. In a matter of months our lives totally changed. Where we once spent up to three months at a time working away from home in different countries, we now only went where he could join us. Additionally, the amount of time we would leave him alone in the house drastically reduced, so our lives had to adapt to only being away from him for a few hours. This dependency meant we were thinking of him 24 hours a day, and that made the thought of losing him seem incomprehensible.

It may or may not be relevant to say that when we had Jake we had no living children, and had experienced devastating baby loss. He was our only dependant and our only focus was on each other and him. I would love to say here that the fear of losing him was worse than the reality of the loss we felt when he died, but that would be a lie. The fear didn't prepare me, it didn't train me to cope when he was no longer here. When he died the world stopped spinning and for a while it lost all purpose.

I'm tempted to say here that this wouldn't even make sense to someone who doesn't love animals, but I'm assuming that anyone reading this book 'gets it'. When Jake died I honestly felt like my life was over, done, complete. I thought I would never smile again or find joy in anything. I was wrong, of course, as joy and meaning returned as I moved through grief, but for some time I felt like I was sitting in a dark, black hole devoid of all grace and hope.

So, what is the lesson? Where am I hoping to land this chapter? I think my hope is to show you we can't prepare ourselves for loss – well, I certainly can't, and I know many others are the same. By leaning into fear, we convince ourselves that we are doing pre-emptive work on our grief journey, but what we are actually doing is robbing ourselves of joy in the moment. We are surrendering our peace and handing it over to fear and control. I wish I had stopped myself counting down the days and had spent more time embracing each 24 hours that Jake was here. Instead of shedding tears because he would one day be gone, I should have enjoyed the peace and joy that came from having him here, in the now. Perhaps this is one of the gifts our pets can bring us. Maybe they are here to teach us that everything good doesn't need to last forever.

Jesse

To go from 'She's the healthiest 13-year-old I've seen' to 'She has weeks rather than months' in the space of six months is heartbreaking by anyone's standards. When you are child-less, infertile, and waiting for IVF funding, and she's the closest you have to a baby, it's beyond comprehension.

In 2006, my life changed wildly and irreversibly. Jesse was our first Siberian husky, and my first dog. She had been abandoned by her owners and had had no human inter-action or walks for around four months. We read all we could get our hands on about huskies, decided we were mad, and adopted her anyway.

Huskies are much like toddlers – stubborn, independent, intelligent. I spent months wondering what on earth we'd done. She was clearly a daddy's girl . . . and Daddy was away a lot with work. Battles of wills ensued. She needed to go into her run when I was out. She disagreed. I had to rig up a pulley system to get her in there long enough so I could get out and shut the door. She was strong; I dam-aged my wrist taking her on a mammoth three-hour hike. She bunny-hopped down the road on normal walks. She hated small yappy dogs but adored her besties Blossom and Anzac.

But we loved her. And we had made a commitment.

Jesse opened up my world. I joined a group known as Husky Heaven and found my crew. Most of the group members were in the US, whereas we are in New Zealand. Here, pet Siberians were few and far between at the time, most were for racing or showing. In the US they were much more popular as pets. Over posts about behaviour issues, funny stories, heartbreak and camaraderie, we became not just friends, but family.

Having Jesse helped me find my passion. Since adopting her, we have been involved in husky rescue – fostering, transporting, administration, cleaning and feeding. I've talked to many would-be owners, letting them know the reality of the breed. We've started a local club for Siberian husky owners and organised monthly get-togethers. I compiled and wrote a weekly breed newsletter for a website. And now, three years after her death, I'm decorating my baby's room in a Siberian husky theme.

You see, one of Jesse's top qualities (and why she was so special) was her love for children, especially babies. Any time she saw one, she had the goofiest look of adoration on her face. Some friends came to stay with their nine-month-old baby, the first time we'd had a baby to stay. Jesse plopped herself outside his room, and every time he so much as farted in his sleep, she would whine to let us know. After that, any time someone came to visit with their baby, Jesse would sit down as close as she could get and sniff, stare, and simper over said baby.

When Jesse was 11, we discovered we would need IVF to have a child. As well as my own need for a child, one of my greatest wishes was to give Jesse a human baby 'of her own'. For an 11-year-old, she was healthy as an ox, and everyone who met her was astonished to learn her age. She flew through every one of her yearly check-ups. But we could still tell she was slowing down. Still, I had every hope that she would still be alive to meet her new sister or brother.

Siberian huskies are known for their intelligence, and she was no exception. I taught her 'sneaky sneaky', and she could almost literally tiptoe into the bedroom and on to the bed without us noticing. Her favourite place to sleep was between us in bed, and some nights she could wriggle her way in there without us realising. My husband and I would have friendly arguments over who got the soft side to spoon, and who got the kicky side (her feet). She loved hiding her cookies around the house, and air-burying them. One day, I walked past as she was burying one quite aggressively. I said to her, 'You're going to have to bury it better than that.' She looked around her, walked over to the pile of laundry waiting to be washed, grabbed a pair of my husband's socks, and carefully placed them over the cookie to hide it.

In early 2018, we'd recently lost Jesse's brother, our other Siberian husky Tikaani, but he had been unwell for years, so it wasn't overly surprising. We began to notice Jesse was appearing confused when she entered a room. I suspected doggy dementia. There were some other symptoms as well, so we booked into the vet. The night before her appointment, we found a tiny lump on her side.

It wasn't dementia. Our 13-year-old baby girl, who just months before had passed her annual check-up with flying colours, was riddled with tumours. She had weeks left. All her other symptoms were related to the tumours. Half her belly was filled with them. At her age, they didn't recommend surgery or chemo. Even if they had, we wouldn't have subjected her to that for what would feasibly be fewer than a couple of extra years. We took her home and vowed to make her last few weeks as fun as possible. Her appetite was decreasing, so she only got her favourites – chicken nuggets and dog roll. We took as many photos as we could, and just spent time with her. It was the middle of winter, and her belly was naked from the ultrasound, so I bought her a new bed. The stubborn wench still insisted on sleeping on the cold concrete.

When she was diagnosed, you couldn't tell by looking at her that she was full of tumours. But three weeks later, she looked like she was about to drop a litter of 10 puppies. We decided at that point, when she could hardly stand and had lost the spark from her beautiful eyes, to let her go.

Holding her as she left us, my heart literally ached. As I leaned over her prone body, I felt an intense wave of guilt: for not having a baby for her to simper over, for not finding a miracle to keep her alive and healthy. I wasn't ready to lose my favourite girl, my only child.

Walking in the front door after work, I would look for her and wonder why she wasn't greeting me. Then came the crash of grief when I remembered. We would find her cookies buried in obscure corners and random boxes for over a year. Each find would break my heart again. Three months after her passing, when our foster dog showed some negative behaviour aspects, I again mourned the loss of my bulletproof girl.

Two years later, when we were faced with the devastating loss of our first human daughter at only 30 weeks, Jesse's loss actually helped me cope. I felt that Jesse would be Romilly's guardian angel, and would be delighted to finally have a baby to care for. The urns containing Jesse's and Tikaani's ashes form an honour guard beside Romilly's ashes, and I know they are all together, causing mischief and mayhem the way huskies and babies are wont to do.

2

Dealing With the Practicalities Of Pet Loss

When you're dealing with your grief, it can be hard to get your head around the practical matters that you'll have to consider, but here are some pointers that I hope will help. Especially when you may feel confused, or exhausted, turning to these practical reminders from those who have been through the same experience may help to make things feel a little easier.

Choosing Burial or Cremation

There are four main options for people to consider:

* ⋆ Communal cremation
* ⋆ Individual cremation
* ⋆ Burial at a pet cemetery
* ⋆ Burial at home or another place (for any public space you need to get written permission from the authorities or landowners)

Some of the choices you make may be dependent on cost, while others may be based on what you feel emotionally comfortable with. Take time to make your decision so you can be certain it's right for you and your family. For instance, you might not want to bury your pet in your garden if there's a good chance you'll be moving house in the next few years.

Cassidy

It was a cool Saturday in September when I met Cassidy. He was a fuzzy little guy with grey, scrappy, uneven hair. He wasn't my first pick. As a matter of fact, I thought he was a little ugly. But his energy was unmatched. His personality was unique. And when he ran, he hopped a little. And that is where Cassidy got his name – after Hopalong Cassidy.

Cassidy was my birthday gift after losing my pet of nine years to diabetes. We bonded right away. Cass, as he was called for short, came home with me and thus began our life together. Little did I know at the time, Cass would become my support system; the one constant in my life for the next 14 years.

As soon as I graduated from college, I received my first job offer. It was six hours away. This was our first move. I accepted the job in a little town in Iowa. Cass and I found a cute little apartment on a busy downtown street. We were there for five months before I was offered another role in a small town in Colorado. So, we were back to packing a moving van and heading west.

While living in Colorado I decided to foster for a cat charity. I did this so Cassidy could have a playmate, and so I didn't have to commit to another animal on the off chance that Cass didn't adjust to having another pet. However, he did well with most of the foster cats.

Our next move was Wisconsin. I continued to foster, and the fourth litter I fostered brought Zeek into our family. Cassidy really took to this little, white, rambunctious kitten with grey spots. Zeek was four weeks old when he came to us and Cassidy was incredibly patient with him, playing with him and cleaning him. I knew that Zeek was going to be the perfect fit for our little family, so I adopted him.

Our many more moves took us to Upstate New York, Minneapolis, Fargo, and Las Vegas. Vegas would end up begin Cassidy's last stop. And it was where I probably needed him the most.

Cass was my shoulder to cry on through my many break-ups. He was there for me when I left my boyfriend while living in Las Vegas. I left him overnight while he was on a weekend trip over Labor Day weekend. He was an alcoholic. He was abusive. And I needed to leave. That night, I phoned my cousin and said, 'I need you to come now. I'm leaving.' And he was there within minutes. We packed my things into his truck in an hour and a half. And I was out.

Cassidy always knew when I needed him. He would nestle up next to my body and purr. And, in those moments, when sadness would overcome me, I was grateful to have such a beautiful creature in my life that loved me so much.

Cassidy also served as my support during a traumatic injury that prevented me from walking. I had injured my back the day before Thanksgiving in 2009 and I spent the next 16 hours on the floor of my apartment in pain, unable to walk. It's pretty crazy how animals can sense pain in their owners. Cassidy circled around me as if to protect me. He would sniff me and meow like he was checking in on how I was doing.

The next few months of recovery were tough. I spent a lot of time in bed or lying on the couch because my mobility was limited. And, inevitably, both Zeek and Cass would curl up on me or next to me.

In the last few years of his life, Cassidy started to lose weight. It was so slight and gradual that you didn't even notice it. The vet discovered he had kidney issues.

Las Vegas was the last place Cassidy lived. I remember so clearly the course of events on the day he left this earth. I had returned from a Christmas break visiting family on 26 December. When I arrived, it looked as though Cassidy was emaciated, though I had only been gone two days. I knew something was wrong and, instinctually, I knew it wasn't good. I was able to get him in to the vet two days later.

It was early in the morning when I took him in. Cass seemed to know. As I was putting him in his kennel he struggled more than usual. He was weak and frail. I feared the outcome. The vet kept him for testing and sent me home. 'We will call you when we know something.'

When I arrived back home, I sat in my car and bawled. I wasn't ready to lose him. But, then again, are we ever?

The call came. It was grave. His kidneys were pretty much shot. And it was time. We made the decision to euthanise. I sat with Cass in the room before he was euthanised, and I cried and cried. All these memories flashed before me: the first day I saw him, when I brought him home, our drives across country, Saturday mornings cuddling, his favourite toys . . . all amazing memories. But when you know you won't be able to experience any of these moments any more, it leaves a giant hole in your heart.

Cassidy had left me and Zeek. I had also decided, at this time, that I needed to leave Las Vegas. I had lost too much.

My one regret is not having Cassidy cremated. The vet clinic worked with a local pet cemetery to have the deceased pets located there. In the weeks leading up to my departure, a lot of guilt had set in. I'd be leaving Vegas and Cassidy would not be with me. White roses grew in the area where the pets were located. So one day I thought, I'm going to go to the cemetery and find the rose that is 'him'.

Before arriving, I thought it would be hard to figure out which rose represented Cass. But, upon arrival, since it was winter, there were no roses blooming. And I was devastated. I sat on the bench and started to sob.

I got up and began walking, and miraculously there was ONE rose that was blooming. And I knew it was Cass sending me a message. So, I took that rose. I preserved it. And I still have it today.

Zeek passed several years later, and the rose currently sits next to his ashes. He had a tumour in his throat and it was inoperable.

The tragedy with pets is that it's almost guaranteed you'll lose them. But you can't help but pour all your love into them. And that is what makes life with pets beautiful.

Having a New Pet After Loss

It's always hard to even consider having another pet when one has died. People often fear that the world will think they are replacing their pet, and that the moment a new animal is present the grief somehow miraculously vanishes.

Let's start by saying no pet can ever be replaced, just like people can't. Every animal and person have their own space in this world, and they are irreplaceable. One can, however, have a need to have a pet companion and when an animal dies this void will need to be filled. A new pet won't fill a previous space, it just creates a new space that is unique to them.

Pets can make a house feel like a home. They can bring meaning and purpose to life. Perhaps most importantly, they can be a trusted companion and confidant and make a person feel needed.

Following our dog's death our home felt so empty. Jake was such a big presence, he filled every room with energy and life. He had beds everywhere, toys strewn all over the floor, and he was extremely demanding of our time. When we went home following his death our house no longer felt like home. If I'm honest, it was agonising to sit in that space without him in it. That was probably why we jumped in the car and drove to the top of Scotland. We didn't know where to go, but we wanted to escape. We hoped we could escape the pain, we hoped that the further we drove the further we would be from the agony. Did it work? No, of course it didn't – the pain, the loss, the raw agony went with us. Every mile we drove showed us we were unable to run, to hide, to escape. What that journey did teach us was the power of weeping. Neither of us held back; the tsunami of tears felt endless. At points we would wail and scream, at other times we would quietly sob, but with no eyes judging us we felt free to express our raw pain. It may sound overly dramatic to some, but those days of driving and the weeks after really were the dark night of my soul.

On reaching the top of Scotland we decided to turn the car around and head home. I didn't want the vet to call to tell us Jake's ashes were ready and us not be there to collect them. When we arrived home, I remember walking through the door and wailing on the floor. I lay on his bed and smelled his scent. That doggy smell that prior to his death I'd spent my life trying to eradicate from our home with scented candles and room fragrance, I now wanted to hang on to for dear life. I felt that was all I had left of him; his bed and possessions, the dog hair that he'd shed just before he became suddenly ill and died within two hours . . . that's all I had left, and I clung to it.

The following days were filled with despair and my memories of them are pretty foggy. What I acutely remember is praying to die every night, because the thought of waking to endure another 24 hours was pretty incomprehensible. I also couldn't sleep in our bedroom, where Jake used to sleep at the end of the bed, so we slept in our guest room. Then, on one bleak spring day, I said to my husband, 'I think we need another dog.'

I knew I needed to have an animal's presence in our house if it was ever going to feel like a home again, and I knew that we could offer another dog a safe haven, just like we had offered to Jake. So, we got dressed and set off for the dogs' home. We walked up and down those kennels, weeping and muttering under our breaths that we just wanted Jake back. None of the dogs were the right one for us. We contacted another kennel and some dog charities and within the week we heard of a spaniel who had been abandoned on a puppy farm. A charity had rescued her and placed her in a foster home, while they looked for a new forever home for this high-energy but scared dog. As soon as we met her we knew we needed her as much as she needed us, and we brought her home. It took us a good few weeks to truly bond with her, but I knew that Jake would have wanted us to do this. We had rescued him once from a life on the streets, and it felt that by adopting this neglected dog we were doing something in his honour.

I would often tell myself that Jake would want us to love her as much as we'd loved him, and this helped me adjust to the new reality of our situation. Our beautiful springer spaniel never replaced Jake; she was just the sibling we would have loved to have had alongside him. A couple of years on our hearts still grieved for our boy, but our house once again felt like a home, and we were just profoundly grateful we'd had that time on earth with our four-legged gift.

'A home without a cat – and a well-fed, well-petted and properly revered cat – may be a home, perhaps, but how can it prove title?'

Mark Twain

Kitty

Nearly two years since her passing the pain still brings me to tears. It hurts as much as the passing of my sons and my mum, because Kitty was part of our family for 16 years.

I can tell you in all honesty that I plunged into very deep blues if not depression. Yes, I have cried myself to sleep, and there is hardly a day when I don't think of her, particularly when I am struggling health-wise and feel a need to be loved like she loved me.

I must be honest and say that if were not for my strong acceptance of a life beyond and that she is waiting for me, it would be so much harder to cope with. I am not sure how others without such faith cope, for without that I would have nothing, just an ending.

I have a rose planted in our garden for Kitty along with a stone with the words 'In Loving Memory' on it. I stand there and speak words of love to her, but each time I do I feel the tears start to flow because I long for her to be here with me.

I never thought that I would ever write such words, for what some would call 'just a pet', but then anyone who has a pet knows they are so much more than 'just an animal'. They are family members, and the pain of their passing is equal to the passing of any human loved one.

We found our cat at a rescue shelter. She had been returned to the shelter twice and was a frightened little girl who wouldn't come out, so we almost missed finding her. Much to the surprise of the staff this frightened little girl came to me and from that moment on a bond of love was formed. I thought I was saving her – it turned out she saved me.

Within months that same timid girl that we named Kitty became a bossy cat with the loudest purr I had ever heard.

Life continued with this new member firmly imbedded in our family.

I started having counselling to help me process the childhood abuse I had been victim to. This was a very hard time for me, as it meant reliving the horror of what had happened to me. I would often break down, and Kitty would always be there to comfort me, her purrs would instantly calm me. If I needed space she knew that too, and would keep away until she knew I was ready to be approached. Throughout all the storms she was there. I believe Kitty taught me how to love, because she loved me after being hurt by previous owners and rejected and cast aside, yet she trusted and loved openly and freely. Her story was similar to mine and through her example this is something I have learned to now do.

I never thought of her as getting old, but she was doing so and my beautiful little girl became a frail old lady of 18 years in the blink of an eye. Sadly, she developed a kidney infection and so we had to make the heartbreaking decision to ease her passing as she was just holding on, doing her duty to care for us, not thinking of herself.

We have another soul friend now, a little boy kitten named Horus whom we also rescued. Not a replacement, because you cannot replace that which has gone, you cannot replace a mother with a mother for you only have one. This is the same with Kitty, she will always be our girl and now Horus will always be our boy.

Sadly, many in society see animals as pets and nothing more. They don't know or understand the pain and real heartbreak of pet loss. Then there are those of us that do understand. We face the same obstacles: no cemetery, no place of memorial where we can visit and sit. We are offered no time off work when we are broken, we just have to cope as if nothing of any importance has happened.

I don't feel I coped very well after her loss; perhaps some would expect more of a strong-looking man, but I am not ashamed to have grieved. I grieved because I loved and that little cat was part of my family and I will miss her forever.

Returning to Work

Returning to work after any type of loss can be petrifying. Loss changes you, yet when people return to work they are often expected to be back to their old selves, which can be challenging. I think there are basically two types of people: one that needs to return to work after a loss, as working actually helps them keep going; and one that just wants to hibernate from the world, so work is the last place on earth they choose to be.

Sadly, most people are not entitled to any paid bereavement leave after the loss of a pet, so if you feel you do need time off your GP would probably need to sign you off work on compassionate grounds or possibly due to stress. The important thing is to take time off if you feel you need it (and a lot of people do). People need time to recover emotionally, and only you know how much time you feel you need or want to take off work.

A note for the self-employed: I know this advice will come down to finances, and whether your work and clients will wait for you to return to work – sometimes jobs don't allow for any leave, and that is just something that has to be accepted – but if you can take time off, please do. Be a kind boss to yourself, and force yourself to look after your physical and emotional needs.

A few practical tips for returning to work

* Prepare in your mind what you will say to work colleagues about your loss. Just having a set answer can help you deal with that unexpected conversation in the office or car park.
* Don't be surprised if you feel physically exhausted when you return to work. Keeping in control of your emotions is physically taxing, so add this to the daily physical tasks of your job – it makes sense that you may feel so drained.
* Ensure you have as many breaks as you can. If you can take time to go for a walk, or just go outside in the fresh air, do it. Take your lunch break and coffee breaks, even if you normally just power through – your mind and body will need these times to regroup.
* For the first few days following your return to work, don't make evening plans; use your evenings to relax and process your thoughts and, importantly, to sleep. The world can quickly feel overstimulating, and you need to give your mind time each day to chill out.
* Eat healthily. The right foods can help you regain your strength so it is important to eat a balanced and healthy diet while grieving. Foods that maintain your blood glucose levels will also help you feel more emotionally stable.

'What greater gift than the love of a cat.'

Charles Dickens

Phoebe

We got our beautiful cocker spaniel Phoebe in 2012. She was only 14 weeks old and we instantly fell in love with her and her gentle temperament. Over the next nine years she brought us so much joy, she gave me unconditional love, and I didn't know love like that existed in life! She would know when I was upset and she was a great comfort to me when things weren't always going well at home. She had a sixth sense it seemed and would put her head on my lap and this would always make me feel better.

I loved coming home from work and her looking out of the living-room window at me as I pulled up. She knew the sound of my car and would be so excited to see me, bringing me a slipper, shoe or toy, or whatever she could find every time! It was the best part of my day and I would hate being late as this would mess up her routine!

When Covid hit in 2020 I got to spend so much more time with her, taking her for extra-long walks and having extra cuddles. She got me through a very tricky time mentally as I am such a social butterfly and was unsure how I would cope with not interacting with friends and family. She was my purpose and thanks to her I got through it, and she loved having me there all day. She would often lie right next to me on the floor while I was working from home. In hindsight, Covid gave me so much more precious time with her and I'm so glad in a way, as little did I know what was around the corner.

In 2021 Phoebe started to get sick and she seemed extra tired. I took her to the vet's and they said she may have eaten something in the park so gave her medicine. I thought she recovered a little following treatment, but by the following month she was struggling to eat and was getting slower and slower on the stairs. The vet suggested she come in and go on a drip for the day to flush anything nasty out of her system, and he also wanted to scan her. I got a call late in the afternoon to say they had sadly found a tumour on her spleen.

It all happened so quickly. In my heart I desperately wanted her to come home with me but I knew I couldn't let her suffer. Because of Covid we had to say our goodbyes in the car park. The vet brought her out to me and she was her normal waggy-tail self, wanting to get in the car to go home – it was utterly heartbreaking. Seeing her walk back in with the vet and knowing what her fate was going to be will be etched in my memory forever. It felt so wrong to say goodbye to her in this way; I longed to hold her as she died.

I can honestly say I have never experienced grief like it. I was inconsolable, my baby was gone, I cried for days and had to have time off work because I couldn't function. I didn't cry half as much for my beloved father-in-law who had passed in the November – this grief was so different.

I felt so guilty for making the decision to put her to sleep, and still regularly ask myself if I did the right thing. How was it my right to end her life? She loved me so much and I loved her. Everything reminded me of her! She always slept on top of the covers between me and my husband, she had to be touching both of us, and I still leave a gap for her even now. I can't walk through the park as it reminds me too much of our many walks together. She is missed so much and I still cry most days over her. All of my family and friends loved Phoebe too and they were all just as devastated as we were when she died.

The garden still seems so empty without her in it. She left a huge gap in my life and I do find it hard to talk about her without crying. It does get a little bit better with time, but I think the grief is so much worse because we were all she had. I really hope we gave her the best life possible. I know we probably spoiled her far too much, but I wouldn't have had it any other way.

Social Media

Many people will tell you that they have a love-hate relationship with social media at the best of times, let alone when they are going through any type of bereavement. My personal belief is that it can be a great tool for disseminating news and expressing feelings one may be experiencing, and it can also play a key role in bringing like-minded people together. That said, I am also acutely aware that it can make some feel very alone and judged.

The problem with social media is that if a person is seen to share 'too much' personal information they may be judged as attention-seeking. On the flip side, if a person does not share enough honest feelings, others may assume they are emotionally fine and much-needed support may not then be forthcoming.

So, what is the right balance? This is something only you can determine and a lot will depend on who you are connected with on social media. If it is just family and close friends, you may feel social media is a good way to communicate your news; if you have a much wider social-media audience, you may want to be a lot more selective.

Choose whether you want to make a statement about your pet loss on social media. Some people hate having to keep repeating the news to everybody, and if you feel like this then a notice on social-media platforms may be a good option for you. Before you post your message, though, consider your audience. Do you just want to let everyone know the news: e.g. 'I'm very sad to tell you all that our beloved dog x passed away last night'; or do you want to let them know more about how you're feeling and how you'd like them to treat you: 'I'm pretty devastated at the moment so please understand if I'm not very responsive.'

Do be aware that some people respond on social media without properly engaging their brains, so at times people may post insensitive comments and responses. It is really hard to gauge people's intentions and emotions on social media, so try to read comments and remarks with eyes of grace, and choose to think the best of people, rather than immediately taking offence. I understand this is easy to write and hard to do, but the last thing you need right now is to be carrying feelings of resentment.

If you want to keep people informed on social media but you don't feel emotionally capable, ask someone you trust to look after your accounts for a few days or weeks. They can then post your messages and respond to comments (and also delete any comments that they think you may not appreciate). Consider starting a group chat, where you can post one message to a select few family members or friends; it can be so much easier to post one message to 10 people, rather than saying the same thing over and over again.

Be aware that forums and chat rooms may not be a helpful environment for everyone. In my experience, these places can often bring together a lot of people who are hurting, and they can quickly make people feel lost, scared and fearing for the future. Of course, there will be the exception and you may stumble across some like-minded new friends, but I always suggest one-to-one support is a lot healthier and more personal.

Follow supportive social-media accounts and pages – my Instagram and Pinterest accounts, for example. I post on these in a bid to help people feel less alone and more understood. By sharing posts from these pages, you can also let your friends and family know how you are feeling without having to find your own words.

'When my dog Buster died, I couldn't get over it. I was in bits.'

Paul O'Grady

My top tips

* Be cautious what you post.
* Try not to be offended if people don't respond in the way you would like, or if they don't respond at all.
* If you want specific people to know your news, ensure they know by sending them a personal message, as it's easy to miss posts on social media; also, some people who are especially close to you may feel offended to hear news about loss on social media at the same time as everyone else.
* Be prepared for people to tag you in on any story or news item they see on pet loss. It is often people's way of showing you they are thinking about you and what you are going through.
* Most social-media platforms now allow you to 'mute'

or 'unfollow' people's daily news and posts, and you may want to consider doing this with particular people. If hearing certain news is going to bring you any feelings of hurt or frustration, choose not to look at it; it won't help you, or help your relationship with them, so just mute their news feed (on Instagram) or unfollow their news (on Facebook). They won't ever know you have done it, since you still remain as a friend and follower.

* Try not to compare your grief or your story with other people's. Social media is a hothouse for this and comparing your walk through grief with another's isn't helpful or healthy. This is your walk – so yes, be encouraged by people and use social media to feel less alone, but if someone's posts are making you feel more isolated or causing you additional pain, don't torture yourself by reading them.

Sandy

I have recently lost my very nearly 13-year-old Labrador, Sandy. We have had her from when she was seven months old, when my daughter was just one, so she has never known life without the dog.

I grew up with cats and so wasn't bothered about having a dog, it was my husband that pushed for it. When she first arrived, I would not allow her upstairs and I very much had the idea that she was just a dog. She soon proved me very wrong! Within months she was upstairs and on the bed with us and was as much one of our children as my two daughters are.

I still always classed her as my husband's dog, although she was part of the family. I was the one who disciplined her and my husband was the one who played with her and cuddled her. She then accidentally got pregnant by my sister's dog and had a beautiful litter of puppies. She was an amazing mom and we ended up keeping one of her babies. As she got older, we realised that we would need a third dog for a short time so that Sandy's daughter could have a companion when we unfortunately lost Sandy. This acquisition happened sooner than planned when one of Sandy's other daughters then got pregnant and had a small litter, so we then had Sandy's granddaughter. All three of them then filled our home with love for two years.

Sandy had always been a very strong-willed madam that knew what she wanted and liked to show she was boss. Some of the things she did were very subtle and others were hilarious. The other two dogs always knew who was boss and sometimes so did we.

Unfortunately, Sandy decided to do a lot of the big things while my husband was working away. She gave birth the night he was leaving for eight weeks so I had to take care of her litter by myself while working full time and taking care of my children. Years later she suddenly became ill and we found out that she had an infected womb and I had to take her for an operation to remove it before it exploded; this again was just after my husband went away. About two years after that we started to see a lump grow in her stomach. This was during the height of the pandemic, so I could only send pictures to the vet's. They quickly took her in and we found there were actually four lumps, some of which were fine but some were cancerous and required surgery.

She then absolutely blew us away. One of her wound sites started dying off and all we could do was let it open itself up and then let her naturally heal herself. For four months we slept downstairs with her, we changed her dressings and we watched her take it in her stride and just let her body heal. She was 12 years old then. This was a big operation for a young dog, never mind a senior citizen, yet she just didn't seem to realise anything was wrong. After the operation her breathing went a little funny but the vet told us that it was nothing to worry about.

The morning before she passed my husband was once again working away. Before I went to work I took all three dogs outside to go to the toilet as normal. Sandy, being an old lab, was a little unsteady at times on the laminate flooring but this time she really lost her feet and it panicked her. As she got into the garden she collapsed and couldn't breathe. I rang work and told them I couldn't come in and then got her to the vet's. By the time we got there she was breathing better but they took her in for a quick check and said to bring her back in the morning for a full check after giving her an easy night. I slept downstairs with her and in the morning she was much more our beautiful girl again, so I went to the vet's feeling very positive. But as they took her into the vet's she collapsed again, to the point where they had to put her on oxygen to keep her alive. They then told me that she was in too much pain and the kindest thing was to put her to sleep.

I have never felt pain like I did in that moment. My husband was away, my children thought I was bringing her home and I had seen our wonderful fur baby collapse multiple times and I knew she was in pain. They told us that they believed the cancer had come back and gone into her lungs. I knew what the right decision was, but I felt so guilty on so many levels for that decision. We all knew she was getting on in years and may not have long left, but this was too sudden, too painful. I rang my husband and we made the decision to let her go. They allowed me in and thankfully she was off the oxygen and breathing by herself by then, so she was at least more comfortable.

Once she was gone I just sat with her and held her; I didn't know how to leave her. The vet agreed to keep her until the local pet crematorium could collect her, because one way or another, our baby HAD to come home! I then had to go home and tell my children. I cried before I went home so that I could try to be strong for them. The next couple of days I struggled to function. At some times having the other two dogs hurt because I still had to feed them, I still had to walk them, without Sandy. But at other times they were a welcome presence because they were still filling our home with love, and walking them got me out of the house. They also seemed to understand, and we could silently grieve together.

Sandy is now back home where she belongs. We still talk to her and her bowl is still out because I simply can't move it yet. It is getting easier, but things still happen that make me cry. We all miss her so dearly. I realise now that as much as I classed her as my husband's dog, I was the first one she met when we rescued her, I was the one she listened to, I was the one she showed her pain to and I was with her at the end. She was just as much my dog and I wish she was still here. She was such an amazing character and I hope that wherever she is, she is still showing everyone who is boss. It would be her birthday soon and we are going to celebrate and get her cake like we always did, and we'll celebrate the joy that she brought to our lives. She was simply amazing and brought joy to everyone who knew her.

Special Occasions and Anniversaries

Until you have lived a full year following a loss, you have no idea what may become a trigger for a wave of grief to hit you (and even after that 12-month milestone new triggers can appear). There are, of course, key occasions to be aware of that may (and probably will) cause new grief layers to be pulled back. These are:

* Birthdays – yours or your pet's
* Anniversaries of the time you adopted your pet
* Pet loss or animal charity awareness days/weeks
* Christmas and other widely celebrated holidays and occasions

I call the moments of grief that hit you from nowhere and metaphorically bring you to your knees 'grief thunderbolts', and if we are always trying to predict and pre-empt what may or may not cause them, we can become constantly fearful of the future. The bottom line is that it is impossible to envisage when they might strike. Even unrelated losses, events or occasions can trigger waves of grief, as anything that taps into similar emotions can cause a fresh wave to hit. You just have to move forwards bravely and deal with your reaction whenever and wherever these thunderbolts strike.

Facing your grief is daring and it's bold; it takes real courage to look loss directly in the eye and still choose to steadily move towards it. Life forces us to face these key occasions, whether we feel ready or not.

What I can say, which I hope will bring you some reassurance, is this: 90 per cent of the time the fear of the event is much worse than the reality of actually walking through the occasion, so try going into events and key dates with an open mind and without preconceptions of how you 'may' feel. Just say to yourself, 'Whatever I feel is okay. If I cry – that is okay. If another grief layer is harshly pulled off – that is fine. If I feel absolutely nothing – that is equally fine.'

Some people choose to mark occasions by doing something special; others prefer to carry on as normal. I encourage you to do whatever you feel is right for you and your family. Remember, this is *your* pet loss journey, your story – you write the rule book.

If you are looking for ideas, here are a few things that I know can help:

* Light a candle on special days
* Hang a Christmas decoration on the tree each year with your pet's name on it
* Plant a tree or plant in memory of your pet
* Donate money or time to a charity or cause in honour of your pet
* Whenever you carry out random acts of kindness, tell yourself that your pet would be proud of you

* Visit a special place
* Read a special book that makes you feel connected to the pet you have lost

Occasions and events can encourage us to show our vulnerability, as we are often forced or persuaded to share our pain and stories with those around us. This in turn helps those who care for us, as they can better understand the pain that is being carried by their loved one (it also often gives them permission to share any pain and grief they may personally be carrying).

One of my favourite quotes is by William Shakespeare, from his play *Macbeth*. He wrote so powerfully about grief.

Give sorrow words; the grief that does not speak
Whispers the o-er wrought heart and bids it break.

So, let me encourage you to choose courage. To bravely reject society's often subtle message to deny one's grief and pain, in a bid not to disturb a happy equilibrium. Be vulnerable, however hard that may seem, because the more open you are, the more you will feel connected to those around you.

Belle

I lost my best friend, Belle, suddenly and unexpectedly . . . well, to say she was just my best friend doesn't give her enough credit. She was my firstborn – born in my heart. She was my family. She was my everything.

Belle spent her entire life with us filling those roles. We shared all of life's special moments with her – our wedding, buying a house, babies, birthday parties, holidays, vacations. There isn't an instance moving forward where she isn't going to be missed.

We had just celebrated her 11th birthday at the park, with her sister (my sister's dog) Aurora. They had a cheeseburger cake, we sang happy birthday, and we went for a short hike in the woods. And now, knowing that she was most likely struggling through that in pain, you could tell she felt so, so loved and I will forever remember her 'smiles' from that day.

Just a few short weeks later, I noticed Belle struggling to breathe. I wondered if the unwavering heat had got to her. But as I waited for her to improve, I grew concerned. Before long, I had her in my car on the way to an emergency vet and, just a few miles down the road, she was gasping for breath. When we got to the vet, she took her inside and immediately started blowing extra oxygen in her nose and mouth. I was scared. I thought for sure the vet was going to tell me that the benign mass that we had been told to 'blindly neglect' on the side of her had finally become a problem. Unimaginably, I was given worse news. She had a second mass growing inside her. And this mass was pushing against her heart and lungs and limiting her airway.

I had a panic attack in the parking lot. At that point, we weren't allowed inside because of Covid-19 restrictions. So, as I was being delivered this news over the phone, my legs felt like jelly under cement. I sat down, sobbing over the phone and trying to wrap my mind around what the vet had just told me. I said, 'I want to take her home.' The vet responded by saying firmly, 'I'm so sorry, but I don't think that is an option. If you take her home, she will suffer. Please come inside to a room so we can discuss our options.'

My sister and brother-in-law were with me and helped me pull myself together enough to go inside. My husband, Joe, was home with the kids awaiting news. So there we sat, in a quiet room, until the vet joined us. She showed us the X-rays and the awful cancer that had taken over what seemed like, to an untrained eye, the entire inside of her body. 'She needs to either be intubated and prepped for surgery (which is painful and expensive) or she needs to be let go peacefully.' I asked that the vet be blunt, and she told us that she'd had no successful recoveries for an 11-year-old dog in what would be equal to Stage 4 cancer in a human. I said, 'So if I choose surgery, it would be a completely selfish choice.' She sadly and genuinely looked at me, and her eyes told me the answer.

At that point, I called Joe and told him he needed to come to say goodbye. In the meantime, I went in the ICU section with Belle and told her how lucky I was to have found her and what a great dog she is and that everything was going to be okay. I even told her that my mom, who had passed three years prior, would be there to greet her.

My husband arrived and we were all moved into a private room. They allowed us time alone with her, but she wasn't on the oxygen at that point, so it was harder for her to breathe. They told us to press the button when we were ready. How do you ever feel 'ready' to press that button? We said our private goodbyes, petted her, loved and hugged her for as long as we could before her breathing again became laboured.

Joe pressed the button and the vet came in and sedated her. As she fell asleep, she laid her head on his arm and I held her paw. We both held her and watched a huge piece of our family slip away as all the milestones she was a part of flashed through my head, just like a movie.

She loved going to Ohiopyle (a beautiful state park located on the southern reaches of the Laurel Ridge in Pennsylvania), chasing crabs at the beach, swimming, being fed a ton of treats from her favourite tiny humans. She went on many adventures with Aurora, and it was clear they always felt fortunate they got to do life together.

I have no words to express my sadness. I feel empty, my home feels empty, and I feel lost without her. I quietly remind myself that at least she is no longer in pain, but that doesn't make my pain diminish.

To celebrate Belle, we have raised money for the rescue centre that we adopted her from. The money is being used to anonymously pay the adoption fee for several dogs to go to their forever homes once they have been vetted by the owner of the rescue. She will be picking families that needed a dog as much as I needed Belle. Starting this fundraiser helped turn my grief into good by focusing my energy on helping at least a few more dogs get to their forever families.

When I was a six-year-old girl, my brother Jeff (who adopted my first dog, Tanya, as a birthday present) told me, 'Any kid without a dog is dogless,' and to this day it resonates in every bit of my heart and soul. My Belle is already so dearly missed and life will just feel incomplete without her. She grew into a family with us and now our family suddenly feels incomplete, without her on earth.

3

Supporting the Bereaved

There are so many ways we can all help the bereaved, and what I would love this book to do is empower you to reach out with confidence to someone who is grieving; whether they have lost a pet or a person I hope this advice will help you.

Let me start by saying the fact that you are even trying to educate yourself on this subject and are researching how best to support someone means *you* are the right person for the job. You want to be the best support you can be, and that makes you one amazing person, so I want to thank you for taking the time to learn about this complex subject.

When I went through loss, I so appreciated those who offered me a hand of support. Some people took to supporting me like a duck to water; others were visibly treading water and trying hard to stay afloat. I appreciated each and every one of them. Those who said amazing things, those who stumbled over their words, and even those who said things that really shouldn't have been said. I loved that they tried; I appreciated that they cared enough to sit with me, even if they didn't feel comfortable doing so. So please don't be worried; just be there whenever they need you, love them, sprinkle kindness on them and be willing to step outside of your comfort zone.

You might think that some of my suggestions as to how to help – or, more specifically, how not to help – may seem quite forthright. I never want people to feel told off, or judged, or panicked, but I do want you to feel fully informed. I want to equip you with the correct empathy tools, and the best way to do that is to tell you some commonly said things that can cause offence, and also some good things to say that can bring comfort.

If you read something in the 'do not say this' section and you have said it, please don't panic. I don't want anyone to feel shame or guilt. All of us can and will have said the wrong things at some point, me included (probably many times a day!), so don't beat yourself up. Instead, say to yourself, 'Okay, I will know what to say next time.'

If you feel you may have caused unintentional pain to someone in the past, you may, of course, want to address that. Just tell whoever you think you may have upset that having read more about grief, you realise that you may have said some insensitive things in the past, and that you're sorry. Saying something as simple as this is the ultimate olive branch, and can bring so much healing to unhealed wounds. You could even give them your copy of *The Pet Loss Guide* as a peace offering.

'Animals are such agreeable friends – they ask no questions; they pass no criticisms.'

George Eliot

Chompy

Back in September 2016, a gorgeous little tri-coloured male guinea pig came into our lives. Chompy was our first pet together, and he chose us! We were regular visitors to the local independent pet shop and he took a fancy to 'chomping' on my husband's fingers, each time we gave him a scratch (he never chomped on MY fingers!). I was keen to bring him home with us, especially after we saw him there for a fair few weeks (I think I wanted to prove I could look after an animal).

My husband and I started trying for children almost a year later. Little did I realise then that we were in for a turbulent ride; after a year of trying, we had no success. Chompy was my 'little boy' who, no matter how hard things got, would always be up for a cuddle and give me licks. He *always* knew how to cheer me up. As my husband and I are shift workers, he was also great company.

Chompy chose a girlfriend, Nibbles (Darth Nibbles, as my husband called her!), on a speed-date at our local guinea pig rescue. She was a beautiful little lady. We had no background information about her, sadly, but within a few days she displayed a few teeth issues (which sadly plagued her for the rest of her short but love-filled life with us). We lost her nearly two years after she came to us, and although I was very upset by her death (and still am, if I'm honest), it was nothing compared to losing our beloved Chompy. He lived a wonderful life in our garden, with his girlfriends (Nibbles, then Chewbacca and finally Munchkin).

In 2020 my husband and I were both furloughed for the majority of the year. When you are not working, and not allowed to socialise with your family or friends, you suddenly realise that having pets enriches your life significantly. Our fertility treatment was paused, which caused me a little anxiety – it constantly felt like one step forward, three steps backward. Chompy, in particular, got more cuddles, treats and attention showered on him than in any previous year, because my emotions kept fluctuating. I'm glad I was able to spend so much time with him. He was a little angel, so placid, and always knew exactly how to put a smile back on my face. People say animals are empathetic and know how their owners are feeling . . . well, he certainly did!

Late in 2020 he started showing his age – slowing down, sleeping more and more and, perhaps most worryingly of all, he started struggling to get back up the ramp from the run to his hutch. We took him to the vet, but all they could suggest was a course of antibiotics and a round of painkillers. The painkillers seemed to help and he started managing to get back up the ramp, so I hoped that he just had a touch of arthritis . . . but things were much worse than I feared.

March 2021 arrived, and one day Chompy came in for cuddles and I spotted him squeaking slightly in pain when he was urinating; there was blood in it. We rushed him into the vet's and they managed to get a very good X-ray of him, without having to sedate him (which is pretty impressive for a guinea pig – the vet was stunned that she didn't have to anaesthetise him). The X-ray showed a massive bladder stone (almost the size of a pea), so we made the decision to have the stone surgically removed (he was never going to pass it by himself). At his age (nearly four years old), anaesthetising a guinea pig was risky. I was overjoyed to bring him home after the operation. He came home looking totally spaced out, and the next day, he started going downhill rapidly – more blood in his urine and, worse still, his appetite vanished and he was passing very small, dried-out poops. We had a brief glimmer of hope when he ate a dandelion leaf (one of his favourite treats) but I knew we needed to get him back to the vet's. We took him in, and they started to bring his temperature up. We went back to bring him home, and another vet came out to say he was improving. He went in to bring him out to us, but then returned to say that while we had been talking initially, Chompy had passed away! I was utterly bereft. I felt so guilty that we had left him with strangers to die. My poor little boy was gone. He was our first pet, and he was meant to be here to meet our firstborn.

It has now been nearly six months since we lost Chompy, and I still cry when I think about him. I feel that I failed him by not insisting on an X-ray when I first took him in, when he was struggling to get back up the ramp. At just under four years old, he should've had another few years with us (guinea pigs can typically live for six to eight years). I'm so grateful for the wonderful memories we have of him. I can't really remember much of what our lives felt like before we had him!

We still have Chewbacca and Munchkin, and in July we welcomed another guinea pig into our herd – little Leia.

The blessing is that when Chompy went over the rainbow bridge, he left a space for another guinea pig to come and live the life of Riley with us. I swear, Leia has the same temperament as Chompy – she even loves pea flakes (the other girls won't even touch them). Chompy filled our lives and hearts with love, and we will never forget him.

My Best Advice

Don't compare

Every journey is unique; therefore, even if you have been through something similar it will be different from the person in front of you, so don't rush to share your story about pet loss, or say, 'This is how I felt, do you?'

Let them tell you their story first in their own words. By doing this the attention will also be kept on the person who's hurting, rather than transferring it to you. If you have lost your dog and they have lost their cat, your stories may have significant similarities, but your journeys through grief will be surprisingly different. Once they have shared, then open up about your story if you feel able and it feels appropriate. At the right time this can be a beautiful and intimate moment. One of my most precious times when I was at the rawest point of my grief was when a friend sat on my bed and shared her own experience of loss; it did make me feel less alone, so choose your words carefully and pick your moment wisely.

Be present

When researching this book, I asked people about the things said to them that caused pain. I received a long list, but one of the things that most people agreed on was that someone just being there, and showing up (even if at times the wrong things were said) mattered more to them than anything.

Having people avoid you, or avoid the topic of pet loss or grief, causes way more pain than stumbling with words, or being a tad insensitive. So be brave and show up, however uncomfortable it makes you feel. Remember, you don't need to say anything; just hold the tissues and tell them you care and want to listen.

Accept you can't fix it

Part of showing up and being present for the grieving is having to accept that you can't fix it for that person. Everything within you will want to make it better for them, – human instinct is to try to relieve another's suffering – but that's not possible when it comes to grief. However much you may want to bring back their beloved companion you simply can't.

If you see it as your job to fix their grief, or to remove it, then very quickly you will feel overwhelmed in your task of offering support, as it is an impossible job and the goal will never be achieved. You will then begin to feel helpless and may start to panic; you may even want to run for cover, as it could feel too hard to be that shoulder to cry on.

To avoid this happening, accept at the outset that you can't fix anything. This acceptance will give you the freedom to just be you; you will realise that all you have the power to do is to listen and to offer support without judgement. I promise you this will be a gift to the person who is grieving.

Never minimise

When we are supporting the bereaved, we need to be careful never to minimise their grief, or oversimplify their journey through loss. I would recommend never to start a sentence with the two seemingly harmless words, 'At least . . . ', as 99 per cent of the time that will be a form of minimising a person's pain. For example, 'At least they aren't in pain any more'; 'At least you can focus on you now'; 'At least you can get another pet', etc.

There is *no* 'At least . . .' in grief support.

Be aware of what they have lost

For the majority of people an animal isn't 'just a pet', it's a beloved family member, and their loss needs to be treated with care and compassion.

'The pain passes but the beauty remains.'

Pierre Auguste Renoir

Merlin

After the disappointing news of our house sale falling
through we took ourselves to the seaside for the weekend.
While we were sitting on the seafront of Weston-super-
Mare we decided to get a puppy instead! We decided we
wanted to welcome a boxer into our family as hubby had
grown up with them. After searching online, we came
across a fairly local breeder, messaged her and went that
afternoon to look at the puppies. We knew we wanted a
brindle one but didn't know if we wanted a boy or a girl.
While choosing, one puppy was in my husband's arms and
fell fast asleep. We knew then that that puppy had chosen
us and wanted to be part of our family. It also helped that
he was quite mischievous! A few weeks later we went to
pick him up, by which time we knew we were going to call
him Merlin. This was mainly to do with the fact that hubby
was an ex-naval helicopter engineer and there is a helicopter called a Merlin. However, he sold it to me by saying it
would be magical for me – like the wizard!

We brought Merlin home and he was honestly the light
of our lives. Within the first year of having Merlin he had
battled his own health issues by having doggy meningitis
and a diagnosed heart murmur from which he made a slow

but great recovery. He also became the reason I continued fighting each day after sad events. I fell pregnant and ended up losing our baby to a miscarriage, and Merlin kept us going with his daft little ways of barking at nothing and putting his head through the cat flap (which we should never have shown him how to do, but it was too funny!). I went on to be pregnant again, and again unsuccessfully; if Merlin hadn't have been around I don't think I could have carried on. I had an ectopic pregnancy in 2013 and I remember when I came home from hospital Merlin lay with me on the sofa with his head resting on my tummy. Merlin honestly made things so much easier and our days much brighter. He loved to sit on the sofa like a little old man watching films with us while we were snuggled under the duvet. We overcame so much with Merlin in our lives, and each time his little face would snuggle up against us and we remembered why we had to keep going.

My mental health took a massive downward turn over the years, with many stays in hospital, but Merlin was always there right beside us, normally giving us his paw for no reason! Merlin would go crazy for visitors and always made sure they knew he was there, often trying to sit on their lap. He loved tug-of-war and would manage to pull us off the sofa! No way was he giving up his toy! Then he would lose concentration and go and bark at something else!

One day we went out to a routine hospital appointment and left Merlin and his new German Shepherd puppy sister in the kitchen as always. When we came back hubby went into the kitchen and thought Merlin was doing his really great guard-dog duties of lying behind the door and not making a sound when someone came in! But this time was different. Merlin didn't move; his 10-year-old heart had stopped beating and he left us that cold, rainy December day.

The loss was like no other. Merlin was our baby, our firstborn, and he always will be. No one and nothing can fill that void in our lives. We carried his body into the lounge and took his paw prints while waiting for the vet to call us back. We then took him to the vet's and had to say our final goodbyes. We couldn't believe our boy Merlin had gone. The house was so quiet. Even with a new puppy! We talked about him every day and watched videos of him and looked back at the many photos we had taken. Merlin left a permanent boxer-shaped hole in our hearts the day he crossed the rainbow bridge. He had somehow always made everything that little bit better; now we had to try and deal with life without him. He will never be forgotten and will always be remembered for helping us through some of the most difficult times of our lives.

Life moves on but the memories live on forever. Take lots of pictures and remember the good times. We are so glad we did. We now have a new boxer puppy, but Merlin will never be forgotten. We often see bits of him in Lenny and it gets us remembering and feeling all over again. Dogs are your family and I'm so glad we have been parents to them. Dogs may be with us for part of our lives but to them we are their whole life.

Helping Children Deal With Pet Loss

What do you tell a child?

Be honest with your child. Yes it may be tempting to tell them an untruth, such as that their pet went to live in a different place, but this can actually make a child more upset. Society often feels a need to protect children from reality, but challenging life events help equip a child to become a kind and compassionate adult, so please don't be tempted to lie.

The language you choose is important, so don't try to soften the words, by saying something such as 'Your cat went to sleep and didn't wake up'. It is better to be clear with your child and state the fact, 'Your cat has died'. When we use softened language such as 'didn't wake up', it can actually make children fear going to bed and falling asleep, so it's vitally important that the correct words are used.

Try not to overcomplicate the situation or overwhelm a child with too much information. They don't need the details. Simply saying the pet was very ill and then died may be enough for some children.

The guilt of bringing pain and grief into a child's life

As parents we have an overwhelming urge to protect our children from any pain and suffering, so it's natural that one may feel guilty if the death of a pet deeply upsets a child. I urge you to remember that death is as much a part of life as birth, and all children need to learn about it. We simply cannot protect our children from experiencing loss. By walking this with them, we are actually equipping them for life.

How to help a child move through grief

Give your child permission to cry about their lost pet whenever they feel the need. Yes, it may be tempting to encourage them to stop weeping and to try to get them to focus on other things, but by doing that you are not allowing them to process the pain they are feeling. When our beloved dog died, I said to my daughter 'Cry as much as you want, the tears will help you move through the pain'. As soon as she knew she had permission to sob as loudly or as quietly as she wanted, she was able to move quickly through the grieving process. After a couple of weeks, she rarely cried about the loss, she was just able to talk about our wonderful pet and smile. Yes, there were days where she would burst into spontaneous tears, but the episodes were short-lived and passed quickly. Most children handle grief so much better than adults as they allow themselves to ride any and all emotions. Our gift as parents is to hold the hand of our child as they journey through the grief.

Honey and Sandy

Honey was, quite simply, the best cat ever! He was a handsome Siamese cat, of good stock, and probably very expensive. He was introduced to our family (two parents, three sons) when we (the boys) were all quite young (I must have been around 10 years old). Honey endeared himself to us with his utter devotion. He never went AWOL, always behaved himself, and didn't seem to have a favourite. He shared himself equally between each of us.

Sandy was a brown dachshund, a pet we had owned for ages. As a vital part of the family, our pets always came with us on holiday: we couldn't properly enjoy ourselves without them.

Honey and Sandy were good if unlikely companions. An evening walk round the garden would involve the whole family, including the cat and the dog, often playing with each other as they followed the rest of us. We didn't realise just how close Honey and Sandy were until the dog had a catastrophic heart failure.

It was a warm summer's day. Sandy was in the garden, Honey was inside. We heard Honey making the strangest noises – unlike anything he had made before. I went to see what the problem was.

Honey was on the bottom step of the stairs, next to a window. He didn't stop the noise, despite my presence or my attempts to comfort him. Then I looked through the window and saw for myself the reason for his upset: he could see Sandy collapsed outside and was deeply distressed. He must have been acutely aware of the seriousness of Sandy's condition, yet – like us – couldn't do anything about it.

It was the saddest of days. We all had to adjust to life without a dog – including Honey, who became king of the castle! Before bedtime he could usually be found in the airing cupboard. After dark, he looked for the warmest bed with a human occupant. I remember one painful occasion when Honey slept on my legs under the sheets, but as he vacated the bed a claw from his front leg accidentally went through my eyelid. It was a memorable moment for both of us, I think.

Honey had a long life, made longer by the fact that our parents refused the vet's advice to foreshorten it when he caught cat flu. Poor Honey really suffered. Towards the end of his long life he could only breathe via a tube inserted into his nose. It was undignified, but kept him going.

So when the end came it was not unexpected. But we could all look back on many years of joyful satisfaction, spent in the company of an extraordinary cat that had some remarkably beautiful attributes.

As a boy, crying didn't seem particularly acceptable. But in private I cried a lot over Honey. He left a void. He had been the best friend possible. That was over 60 years ago, but proves what an indelible mark our pets leave on us.

Frequently Asked Questions

Can you move on following loss?

I often hear people say about those who are grieving, 'They just haven't been able to move on', usually whenever a period of time has passed since the death of a pet or a loved one and the person is still talking about the loss, or showing visible signs of grief.

Grief and loss are not something you simply 'get over', so just because someone is talking about the loss still, or is displaying symptoms of grief, this in no way means they are 'stuck' (although it can happen – see below); it merely means they are processing the loss, and that could be something they do for the rest of their life.

The loss of anyone or anything becomes part of who you are, and you learn to carry the weight of the grief and allow it to shape you into a different person.

How can we help people along their grief journey?

By allowing them space to talk and share. If we try to rush people to process pain, it has the reverse effect and sets them back, so all we can do is walk alongside them and hopefully we will then start to witness them rediscovering their joy.

Can you become stuck in grief?

People often come to me saying their family member or friend is stuck in grief, and asking how they can help them. My first question is always, 'What do you mean by "stuck"?' Just because someone is talking about the pet or person they have lost, it does not mean they are stuck. Just because someone is still weeping and heartbroken, it does not mean they are stuck.

That is how grief works; people are meant to still talk about their loss, and they are grieving healthily if they still communicate their pain.

My worry is for the person who *can't* talk about their pain, and for the one who makes it seem like no loss has even happened.

Having said that, is it possible to ever get stuck in grief? I believe it is.

I would question (and notice I say question, not assume) whether someone was stuck if their loss was a long time ago but they were still finding it impossible to talk about anything other than their pain. I would also consider whether someone was stuck if after perhaps a year they felt it impossible to move forwards in ordinary life because of being consumed by sorrow.

However, there are no set rules and no set formulas when it comes to moving through the grieving process. One plus one doesn't always equal two when it comes to grief.

What can we do if we think someone is stuck?

There is only one thing anyone can do and that is listen to their story. By doing that you will:

* Hear their pain
* Validate their experience
* Show you care

People mostly get stuck because they feel a need to defend their right to be experiencing pain, as they don't feel their story is being heard. They may also want to ensure their pet is being acknowledged and not forgotten. Simply by listening, we can help them unstick themselves.

Can a grieving person achieve closure?

Closure following a loss is as much of a myth as unicorns and fairy tales. You cannot close the door on grief. It is just not possible to put all your feelings into a box, seal the lid and consider it part of the past.

All anyone can do is come to accept what has happened and learn to live with this new state of reality. Compart-mentalising feelings invariably leads to unresolved grief bubbling through at another time in their life, often negatively affecting their physical, emotional or mental well-being.

Does grieving in public help?

Public grieving can help because we can suddenly see we are not alone in our pain. There is a reason we hold funerals, a reason that people from all different cultures around the world gather to remember and celebrate the lives of those who have died, and that reason is that something powerful happens when we stand together. We feel supported. We feel less alone. We feel our loved one has been duly honoured. We feel our pain and loss has been recognised.

Seeing all of this and exploring all of this helps hearts begin to mend, but those who have lost pets aren't usually offered this ceremonial ritual. Instead they quietly bury their pets' ashes or bodies alone. If you have supportive family and friends, I would encourage you to ask them to join you in a private saying-goodbye event, even if this is just in your back garden.

How do we tell the difference between grief and depression?

You won't know this, and often the bereaved person may not even know it. I always look for signs of depression in a person if I know they have suffered from depression pre-loss. Grief tends to come in waves; depression doesn't move, it stays like a black cloud. Grief can trigger depression, and grief can develop into depression. However, mostly grief stays as grief and is not 'depression' at all.

Be careful with how you word questions about how they are feeling and encourage them to share their worries and concerns. GPs are trained to help people determine whether they are depressed, so I would always encourage a person to sit with a doctor and talk about their feelings and symptoms, and then the doctor can advise them on what is best to do next.

A big alarm bell for me would be talk or mention of suicide. There is a *big* difference between someone not wanting to live (because of the depth of the pain they are experiencing and the overwhelming feelings of missing the pet or person they have lost – like I felt when I lost Jake) and being suicidal. It is very common not to want to be here any more – who would want to live in agony daily and see no chance of respite on the horizon? Being suicidal is very different and if someone is considering ending their life or you feel he or she is at risk of this, encourage them to seek urgent medical help and/or encourage them to call the Samaritans or another mental health support charity.

Twiglet

Where does any love story begin?

It begins with the first 'Hello!'

I first laid eyes on Twiglet when she was a four-week-old puppy. I had responded to an advert in the local rag and drove down to Corwall. She chose me. She gazed deep into my eyes with her deep chocolate pools, lined perfectly as though with black kohl. She tipped her charming head to the right and I was lost! I knew then that she'd be mine and I think I also knew that she'd break my heart . . . almost 15 years later she did just that.

Twiglet came to live with me at almost eight weeks old. She was the model dog: intelligent and easy to train. She was a beautiful soul with an amazing character. Of course, I knew she was a dog but, in many ways, she was the child I could never have.

After just two days Twiglet had wormed her way into my bed, sleeping under the covers. Some mornings I'd awake to find her head on the pillow next to mine; I'd smile and feel so blessed.

I hated to be parted from her and if I went away without her, I'd bring her a present back. I would also drive Tracy, my dog-minder, mad by calling several times a day to make sure all was well.

She loved cuddly toys, particularly those with a squeaker, I would leave *In the Night Garden* on the TV for her as she liked the audio – Iggle Piggle sounds similar to a squeaker. I would call her 'Mrs Twiggle Piggle'!

I kept her first teeth in a wooden box made for a parent to keep those from their child.

She was the love of my life . . . but there was a dark side. I was in a very dangerous and abusive relationship. I was prey. Twiglet was my comfort blanket, my reason to survive. So often suicide seemed the only option, but I could never ever leave her. Twiglet adored me, she would follow me everywhere. She was my 'Velcro' dog. Her eyes followed my every move. I made her two promises: the first was that I would keep her safe, protect her at all costs; and the second was that I would never leave her. I kept them both.

My abuser left me when Twiglet was just five months old, and that kept her physically safe. For me, it was just turning life's pages to the next chapter. The abuse would continue erratically for eight more years. He was a very dangerous man, hellbent on destroying me. Twiglet was my saviour.

We were the perfect long-lasting love: two swans floating down a moonlit river, two butterflies dancing in the breeze.

We had many adventures together: she came to work with me occasionally and was even a life model in a children's art class. She loved running on the beach and would skim the incoming tide but never go in the sea. She chased pigeons and squirrels, returning home exhausted to lie on her bed and wait for me to cover her with a blanket. She would cuddle a soft toy and suck the corner of her blanket until I would ask in a silly childish voice, 'Are you being

Baby?' when she would look embarrassed and stop immediately and shut her eyes.

She was an excellent traveller, enjoying car rides. It became much healthier for us to holiday together. She accompanied me to Wales, Cornwall, Derbyshire, Northumberland, Scotland, Somerset and Dorset . . . we were inseparable.

At 13 Twiglet was starting to show signs of old age and was slowing down. Her back became painful. Vets recommended gabapentin and monthly acupuncture, which helped a great deal. Now happily married, slowly I made changes to the home and our daily routine. I began lifting her in and out of the car, I carried her up and down the stairs and I padded up both sides of our bed to assist her getting in and out and to avoid injury should she fall out! Her chocolate-brown face slowly became splattered with grey but she was always so beautiful. She was just so blessed with one of those faces that, though aged, never lost its beauty. Her hearing seemed to vanish so suddenly, but we could still communicate with hand gestures and facial expressions. She was just such a happy dog. She was still my shadow – where I was, so was she. She never lost her love of food, although she started taking a lot longer to eat her dinner and more frequently she would leave a bit. I'd pick her up and kiss her ears and smell her. I loved the smell of her. I loved every hair on her head, every inch of her. I loved the feel of her velvety ears.

One Monday evening in June she seemed a little out of sorts. I carried her upstairs to bed. I struggled to sleep that night, continually checking on her, making sure she was breathing normally. Her back legs felt very cold. I tried hard to gently rub them to warm them up. In the early hours she became a little distressed and got out of bed. I followed her, gently talking to her and soothing her. She was sick. I tidied up and she seemed better after that, so we climbed back into bed and slept.

The following morning, I cooked her favourite minced steak. She ate most of it. I was due to visit my mum, so I kissed her 'goodbye' and, as always, I told her to be a good girl for Daddy. She followed me to the door; I closed it and looked back at her through the glass, looking into her beautiful dark and adoring eyes. I blew her a kiss and left.

That afternoon my husband called and suggested I came home. My heart was thumping – I knew it was Twiglet. She had gone outside to the toilet. After a while my husband went to check on her. He described her as sitting like a statue. On touching her she seemed to lean on him and keel over. I told him to carry her in and lay her on her bed, and that I'd be driving straight home and would be there within the hour. I was. The drive had been torture. I hit traffic, I screamed and sobbed. I yelled at the top of my voice, 'Wait for me! Please!' as though she could hear my pleas.

On arrival I flung myself at her bed. I lay down next to her and kissed her ears. I had to weigh up taking her to the vet's, something she hated in spite of us having a wonderful vet, or allowing her to pass at home. I gave her about an hour as we lay there, her paw in my hand, and I prayed for her not to leave me. She tried to get up and began drooling. I scooped her up and my husband drove us to the vet's. I was seen quickly as an emergency, not by my usual vet but an empathetic professional none the less. The bottom line is that we agreed they should give her an anti-nausea injection and we should take her home to either pass overnight or hopefully show signs of recovery and an interest in food.

We lay together on the lounge floor all night. I held her paw. At times she became distressed and I will spare you the ugly details, the agony of watching a loved one's organs shut down. I prayed that God would take her home but sadly he didn't call her to Heaven. By morning I knew I had to make that decision. I was waiting at the vet's emergency back door at opening time. I didn't want to say goodbye, I could not imagine how I could ever go on without her, but I also knew it was my final act of love to release her from her failing body. The vet had reassured me that even if I offered him a million pounds he still could do nothing to save her. The man who had looked after Twiglet over many years gently and sympathetically helped her over the rainbow bridge in the back of my car as I smoothed her ears with my lips and whispered how much I loved her and asked her to wait for me.

It was so quick.

I felt her take her final exhale and then there was nothing. She was gone.

It was a peaceful passing. I sat with her for about half an hour and waited for the crematorium van to arrive. I carried her to its open doors and laid her on the pet bed in the van's vacant and bare interior. I placed her little toy between her paws and kissed her still warm body one last time. The van departed and I blew her a kiss as she exited the car park.

Grief was overwhelming for hours, days, weeks. It came in waves. I allowed myself to grieve. I received her ashes a few days later and placed them in my bedroom along with a framed photo and pawprint taken at the pet crematorium.

It helps to have them near. I know we will be together again one day.

Twiglet, my best friend: I loved you your whole life, I'll miss you for the rest of mine.

Things Not to Say and Why

I am regularly asked what you shouldn't say to a grieving person. I prefer to focus on the right things to say, but I can also see a real benefit in highlighting the pitfalls and the things that are habitually voiced to the bereaved.

So here goes – buckle up, my friends, and let me take you on a journey of clichés and the reasons why they cause pain.

'Let go'

If you say to someone, 'Let go of the pain' or 'You need to let go of your pet now and just move on', you will be causing deep hurt, and I know that is the last thing you would want to do.

It's not possible to 'let go' of a pet you have loved and lost – emotion doesn't work like that. In fact, love doesn't work like that. Although their pet is no longer living life in the physical sense, the love their owner feels for them is acutely present. The only thing they need you to do is walk with them, help them to carry the load in any way you can, journey with them as they learn to juggle the task of processing grief and pain while remaining present in the world.

'It is time to move on/get over it/stop talking about it'

Grief is not something one 'gets over', and talking about the pain of loss is the best way for people to start to heal, so this needs to be encouraged and never discouraged.

'God didn't want them to stay'/'They are in a better place now they are in heaven'

This is just so painful and insensitive.

Avoid bringing God into the conversation. Whether or not a person has faith, God didn't make this happen and trying to insinuate that their pet is in a better place says their home on earth was not the best place for them, which is hurtful.

'Time will heal your pain'/'Life goes on'

True, at times pain can decrease over time; however, it can also increase. No bereaved person will thank you for telling them that life will get better down the line while they are in the depths of grief, so avoid telling them it will.

Just let them focus on today, as that can seem daunting enough when you are journeying through loss.

'At least they lived until they were a good age'

We've already discussed 'At least . . .' so we know it shouldn't be said at all. Sadly, this is said so often to people who lose an elderly pet. Just because an animal is older it doesn't make the pain and grief any less important. Additionally, just because someone is grieving and devastated that their pet has died doesn't in any way make them ungrateful for the years they had with their companion.

'At least they are out of pain'

Another dreaded 'At least . . .' But again, this is so commonly said to people, especially if the pet who has died suffered from any sort of disease or condition that meant they experienced pain.

No one wants to see their pet suffering and, yes, you would be right to think this is possibly one of the only positive outcomes following the death of an animal who was in agony, but it doesn't help to be reminded of it many times a day when grieving. If the bereaved person is saying it, that is of course totally fine. However, it's often said to try to make a person look on the bright side, and it's much better to let them process the grief they are carrying.

'You are lucky you still have another pet'

Of course, every pet is a real blessing, but having other animals doesn't remove the grief you feel for the pet you have lost.

'Loss is an inevitable part of owning a pet'

Yes, animals dying is a common life occurrence; however, that does not make it less painful, or something anyone should expect.

'You have been through it before, you can cope again'

Just because someone has survived one loss, it does not automatically make them better equipped to deal with it a second, third or fourth time.

Yes, a previous pet loss may have taught them some life lessons or coping skills, but this can never be presumed, and should certainly never be spoken out loud. Every loss is different, and personality, life circumstances, emotional stability, physical health, etc. all play a part in how people cope.

'Once you have another pet your pain will go'

This is entirely untrue, and no bereaved person would ever agree. It should never be thought or communicated. Another pet will never be able to replace the one who has died, and while other animals are an absolute gift and blessing, their presence doesn't take away the pain of losing the pet who has died.

'You're lucky your pet had access to medical care when so many animals don't'

This may be true, but showing someone how privileged we are to live in a developed country with plenty of vets doesn't help their pain. You are just subtly (or possibly not so subtly) removing their permission to grieve.

'My friend lost their pet when they died from *xyz* – that is much worse, isn't it?'

Comparison helps no one. There is no score attributable to grief and loss. Why does one have to be worse than another? Instead, let's stand together and say all loss is horrid, every pet death is traumatic, and every person touched by loss deserves to be supported.

'It's good that they died quickly and didn't suffer as long as *xyz*!'

This is another statement that minimises someone's loss and grief. The length of a pet's illness doesn't change the amount someone grieves.

'In a few weeks, you will feel like a whole new person!'

Positivity doesn't change the reality, and while you might like to fast-forward time so that the person standing in front of you isn't in pain, you cannot rescue them, and you can't say with all honesty that things will be better soon. By even trying to do this you remove yourself from being a trusted and reliable confidant, as it shows a real lack of empathy and compassion to speak with such authority about something you cannot be certain about.

'Maybe if you didn't think about it so much, it would be easier'

Grief can't be denied or avoided. In fact, the more you try *not* to think about it, the more it can overwhelm the brain.

It needs time and space to be processed, so by encouraging people not to think about the loss of their pet, you are doing them a disservice.

While it is possible to get overly consumed with focusing on loss (which of course wouldn't be healthy), the majority of people aren't dwelling on grief; they are simply trying to survive the loss. Their brain needs time to come to terms with the trauma of losing their beloved companion, and unless they give themselves space to focus on their situation, they will never be able to move forwards healthily.

Let me also remind you that there is no 'normal' when it comes to loss, so who can even determine what is 'too much'? Too much to you may not be enough for another person, so we must be mindful not to judge or comment on how any person journeys through grief.

'Maybe this is just a sign that you shouldn't have a pet'

It is hard to believe that this is ever said to a grieving person, but I have heard it being uttered, so I know it happens. It is hurtful, it's thoughtless and it should never be thought, let alone voiced.

'Aren't you feeling better yet?'

This question usually gets asked within two to four weeks of a pet loss – shocking, isn't it? Sadly, if people don't grieve fast enough, the world often makes them feel abnormal for still hurting, for still crying and for still feeling broken. As soon as you say the words 'aren't you?', you are putting an expectation on that person that they should be further on in their journey, and that brings more hurt and pain to their door. Instead, ask: 'How are you feeling today?' Or: 'Have you been able to experience any moments of peace this week?'

'When do you think you will be back to normal?'

I can answer this one for you. Never. People who have experienced loss (whatever the loss) never return to the old them. Loss and grief change you forever, so if you can accept that and then gently help the bereaved person discover it, you will be an excellent support for them as they walk through grief.

Buddy

In the autumn of 2010, I was working in animal rescue when my colleague brought a scared, skinny and traumatised German Shepherd dog into the office. She was taking him to kennels, after he had been discharged from the animal hospital. I took one look at him and, despite being in a totally unsuitable living situation at that time, immediately said I'd take him home. His owner was being investigated for animal neglect but, after several months of fostering this dog – who I named Buddy – I knew that I'd rather risk my job and go on the run with him than return him to the person who had abused him. Thankfully, the owner eventually signed him over and he officially became mine.

For 10 years, Bud was my shadow. It was no secret that I loved him more than anyone or anything else in the world. He gave my life purpose and he made me feel safe. I'd grown up in a rather dysfunctional family, where I'd learned that to stay safe, I needed to shrink into myself and stay quiet, where I'd believed that I had to constantly adapt who I was to please other people, that I was not worthy enough as I was. Bud made me feel that I could be whoever I wanted to be, and he would accept me, love me and never leave my side. Every time I buried my face in his soft fur, it felt like home.

He would gaze at me with such soulful eyes and make me believe that it would all be okay, during times when I lost everything – my home, my health, my job, my beloved horse, friends and family members. When the dark pit of depression threatened to swallow me up, he was the calm and steady presence beside me encouraging me to get back up, to keep going, to find the joy in the small things, like he would find the joy in finding a discarded tennis ball on a walk, or being given a piece of cheese rind, or that first feel of sand between his toes when we went to the beach. If he was happy, so was I. We were a partnership, best friends, soul mates. Someone once asked me what I lived for and I answered without hesitation: Buddy.

As he got older, he was diagnosed with arthritis, which I managed through regular hydrotherapy, acupuncture, laser therapy, massage, and various medications to keep him comfortable. I couldn't contemplate him growing old, and the separation anxiety I'd always suffered from when I was away from him started to worsen, especially as the pandemic hit and I was rarely forced to ever leave him. I did my very best to ward off time and believed that we had years left together. With him beside me, I felt invincible and naively thought that he was too.

Last year, after I had been away for a rare weekend camping trip without him, Bud became ill with what I presumed was just a gastric virus, and I took him to the vet's, assuming that 24 hours on fluids would build his strength back up and I'd be bringing him home again. However, he deteriorated quickly and within 48 hours, on 30 September 2020, I was told he had cancer, with multiple tumours in his lungs and spleen, and that there was nothing they could do. He was so weak he wasn't eating and could barely stand up.

So that is how I found myself having to say goodbye to my whole world. Everyone thinks their dog is special, and nobody is wrong, but my dog was one in a million. He was gentle and kind, with the heart of a lion. Life without him was impossible to contemplate. Yet here I am. My heart is shattered yet brokenly beats on. I am still breathing, although I don't know how.

It is hard to put into words what grief feels like. I once saw love described as feeling like your heart is full of helium. Well, grief feels like your heart is full of lead. But I guess that makes sense, as grief is the opposite of love. One makes you feel light and one makes you feel heavy, but you can't have one without the other. For me, grief feels like gravity is dragging my body downwards, like a magnetic tug towards the ground; like carrying rocks in my chest, a constant feeling of heaviness and pressure; like wading through deep water when I was never taught to swim and when wave after wave of pain is pushing me further under. Grief is navigating an alien world without a map, feeling lost and desolate, bereft and confused, not knowing which way is up or how life can ever begin to make sense again.

I've not slept properly since he left. Fitfully and exhaustedly I am plagued by thoughts, memories, cold sweats and vivid dreams at night, even now he is back home in a handmade engraved urn beside me on my bedside table and even as I cling to his favourite cuddly toy. I wake groggily every morning to a world devoid of colour, to be punched in the gut by that fresh wave of reality. I have tried to throw myself into work, which is all I really know how to do, to focus on a job that means something at a time when everything else seems pointless. Throughout the day though, sitting at my desk where he would normally be lying at my feet, I catch myself looking for him, turning to say hello, reaching my foot out to stroke his back, before the crushing realisation that he is gone.

The problem with the type of grief that losing a pet provokes is that people expect you to be over it almost instantaneously. They tell you that 'you can get another one', as if a soul mate is easily replaceable. I have adopted a new dog now, and I adore her, but does she diminish what I felt for Bud or take away any of my grief for him? No, because she isn't Bud and never can be. The week she came home was when I hit rock bottom. It was the pressure to force a smile, everyone assuming I would be so excited about her arrival when all I wanted was Bud back, to miraculously return like it was the most macabre magic trick or the worst practical joke. It felt as if I was expected to just move on, before I was ready, when I will never be ready because I can never begin to understand or process the injustice and unfairness.

People talk about time, but it doesn't fix this. It doesn't make the ache go away. At best you learn to live with it, and it becomes who you are now. The same way that the one you lost will nestle themselves in the cracks of your heart and you will carry them there, wherever you go, whatever you do, always. Eventually there will be longer moments between the crying, maybe there will even be moments of joy. But, my God, you will still miss them with every fibre of your being, and you will never ever stop.

The thing about loving a pet is that although you know that you are likely to outlive them, you're still not prepared for living without them and you don't stop loving them with every part of who you are. Loss is inevitable if we are to love, and what an empty life it would be if we did not dare to love. I would rather be enduring this unfathomable pain than never have had Bud in my life. So, I am still trying, even if at times I desperately want to give up, even when carrying on feels like a superhuman achievement.

I have learned that you can keep going, long after you think you can't. Right after Buddy died, I felt like I was barely even existing, that I was just going through the motions, just surviving but not thriving. But we must try and seek out those moments of joy in the seemingly unrelenting sorrow, to paint colour back into our grief-stricken, greyscale world, to believe that not only could life one day be worth living again but that, even without the one we have loved and lost – the one we said we lived for – we can still piece together the fragments of this mess and enjoy some sort of a good life. A life that I know Buddy would want me to live.

Proactive Advice for Family and Friends

Having covered what not to say, here comes the positive part – some practical tips on how you can support someone who has lost a family member which happens to be an animal. Prior to being trained and then subsequently working in the field of bereavement care, I remember feeling so confused when I was faced with helping bereaved friends and family members – I wanted to make things better for them, but I didn't know what help to offer. I hope this section makes you feel empowered and equipped to support any broken-hearted people on your path through life.

When supporting a loved one, you need to realise that things can stack up and suddenly reach crisis point, so be aware of some of the typical responses:

Wanting to run away

What they want is to escape the pain, and, in their head, they feel like they can run away from it. Unfortunately, this is not the case, and even if they do travel the grief goes with them. Listen to them, and give them space to express their sadness.

Not wanting to leave the house

Often people find security in their home and can almost become phobic about leaving their house, as the world can feel like a terrifying place. Of course, I would not advocate dragging people outside against their will, but I do always recommend gently encouraging people to step out of their front door regularly. The longer it is left, the harder it can become to do. Little and often is the right approach.

Panic attacks

Some may have experienced these pre-loss, but for others the loss may have triggered their first attack; either way, it is terrifying for the person. Be aware that this isn't something that can just be brushed off – it is the brain's way of saying, 'I can't cope right now.' Gently encourage them to seek help from a professional and chat with their GP.

Lack of appetite/eating much more than usual

Most of the time, people's appetite will return to normal within a few weeks, so encourage them to drink plenty of fluids if they are eating less.

Eating little and often is usually more comfortable for those in the depths of grief, and a great gift is lots of snack packs, as nibbling on food can help the appetite return. If their regular eating pattern doesn't resume within a month, I often suggest a person should sit down and talk in depth with a friend or a professional, to see if verbalising their grief helps.

Wetzel

I'd always heard of the concept of having a dog as a best friend but never truly understood it until Wetzel came along.

Fresh out of college, I was miserable, living on the East Coast of the USA. I was miserable in the way an early-twenties recent college grad whose first job is not working out will be. I felt my life was over and my mom decided I needed a dog. I came home for Thanksgiving and there was Wetzel. He was the smallest, cutest thing I had ever seen. From the first meeting I knew he was going to be my little boy. The first day together we went shopping all over, getting a crate, bedding, etc. I took him with me, and he started to curl up on my foot.

I took him on the plane with me back to my job and that night hugged him all night. I was unhappy but he made me happy. We spent so much time together and even though I was homesick he made the experience a little better. The first night with him I decided we would sleep in the same bed (something my parents never allowed). I felt so lonely being in a new state and away from everything I knew but he made it better. I felt I was starting to become energised and also realising what I wanted in my life. I think he truly helped me put my life into perspective. Any time I would go out with friends I would worry the whole time about him being home alone. He gave me something to come home to.

A few weeks after he came into my world I lost my job. So all those cuddles became constant. Wetzel would make sure I did not stay up too late, barking at me when it was bedtime. I also learned how much he sensed if I was having a hard time. The cuddles were extra-cuddly then.

My dad came to drive me home and then I started a phrase Wetzel would grow to love. As we drove, when he became a little too rambunctious, I would say 'sleepy'. This became my phrase to him. And we always slept together. From day one, he got me through a difficult phase of my life.

Over the years Wetzel and I went through so much. He was there when I thought my life was over (when I lost my first job), when my dad was very sick, through losses of friendships and relationships, and just bad days. I remember those days coming home and crawling into bed. He always knew his spot right against my ribs, under my arm.

He was also there for the celebrations – me getting new jobs, graduating with my master's, meeting my now husband, and every get-together. He would meet any potential date so I could see how they reacted to each other. Friends would ask what would happen if I liked someone and Wetzel did not, and I would answer it would not even be a question. I would tell him about my days, and he was truly my best friend.

Things in my life were going well. My husband and I had bought a home, got married, and added another dog to the house (mainly to help Wetzel). The first night we moved into the house Wetzel ran up and down the stairs nonstop. He had always been a city apartment dog so the idea of having stairs with free roam was amazing. This is one of my favourite memories of him.

Then I had a rough few weeks. My sister was hospitalised with pre-eclampsia, and I would come home from visiting her and hold Wetzel. I knew at this time he was getting up there in age, but he was still my buddy and there for me. When my niece was born, I came home and told him all about it. She sadly did not live a long life. I again leaned on Wetzel as my support.

I knew he was getting older but did not want to believe it. Then, only eight days after I lost my niece, I lost my best friend. I like to think he did not want his cousin Colette to be alone so went up to Heaven to be with her.

This did make grieving hard. I cannot imagine what my sister and brother-in-law went through. They also were understanding and gave me room to grieve for Wetzel. I just had a very hard time allowing myself to. Society disregards the loss of animals and when you put it next to a true tragedy it becomes even more complicated. I was in a fog for the days after, just knowing I wanted someone to talk to again. I still miss him. I especially feel this when things become stressful. I was on a trip for work that was high stress and when I came home, I remarked to my husband, 'I just wish I could nap with Wetzel.' Napping was probably his favourite thing.

Every day I miss Wetzel. He truly changed my life and continues to. I have plans to get a paw tattoo for him and have a large pot that I planted shortly after his death in memory of him and Colette. I know it is a strange concept, but he taught me to just enjoy life and be in the moment more often. I will never meet another dog like my Wetzie.

What to Consider

Please don't be scared about seeing pain and grief up close and personal. Yes, it is hard to see someone you care about upset, but if you were in their shoes you would want the people you love to surround you, and you can be one of these people to them.

Grief can trigger a host of other emotional issues

If someone has issues in his or her marriage/relationships, they are likely to surface at this time, so be aware of this possibility.

Seek to understand more about loss and grief

It is easy to oversimplify loss and almost consider it unnatural, but it is one of the most natural parts of life; there is a time to be born and a time to die. If you can become comfortable talking about the subject of death, you will be able to support the grieving much better.

Don't presume anger is part of grief

Of course, some people may experience a degree of anger in the grieving process; however, many won't, and to assume someone's anger is just part of grief can be harmful to the individual and mean injustices aren't addressed.

Think before you share

When you are bereaved, some information is more painful to hear. For example, 'I can't believe my dog won't stop barking!' This can be a kick in the guts to someone who has just lost their pet, so be aware of this. Grief can make people less patient for a time and also blunter, so think before you speak and be mindful. This doesn't mean you shouldn't share about your life at all. I welcomed news of other life issues or situations when I was grieving; it gave me time to think of someone else, but how it was shared was significant.

Know and accept that the bereaved are likely to get tired more quickly

Grief is exhausting; it uses every bit of the physical and mental energy available to a person, and often that means they spend a lot of their time saying how tired they are. Reassure them that it is normal, and when you see them or do activities together, perhaps focus on things that don't need much physical energy.

Be subtle

Often bereaved people will tell you they forget things all the time and find it difficult to focus; this is just because their brain is in overdrive dealing with the pain of loss. Think of it like a computer having a hundred tabs open on the browser – everything slows down, and sometimes the whole PC needs to shut down and reboot. Offer gentle reminders to those you are supporting to alleviate the pressure, even if it's just by sending a simple text – for instance, 'Looking forward to seeing you tomorrow at 1pm.' Then you aren't highlighting the fact they may not have remembered the arrangement or the time.

It is okay to laugh and smile

One of the things that the bereaved struggle with is allowing themselves to smile without feeling guilty, as they fear those around them will assume they are 'over the loss' if they laugh. It can also feel disloyal to the pet they have lost to smile and enjoy life. I spend my life reassuring the bereaved that it's not only okay to smile, but it's also crucial that they do, as the brain can only handle so much trauma, and it needs light relief and an escape at times.

Bilbo

We have always had cats as a family and when I got married that tradition continued. The year after our wedding my wife Helen surprised me with two cats for my birthday – and she let me choose. I picked the kitten that made a beeline straight for me as I entered the room.

Bilbo, a white moggy with sharp green eyes, was always out and about over at the park chasing seagulls and teasing swans. He was well named, always out having some adventure but always finding his way home again. Out of the two of us he had always gravitated towards me more and most evenings would sit on my lap after work and often lie on my back at bedtime. While I was at home, he often made a point of being home as well and, like a dog, would be waiting for me as I arrived home from work and greet me with a cry and be round my ankles like a moth to a flame.

His daytime friend, our other cat Ginny, was quieter and more cautious, a tortoiseshell furball, she was, as my wife always said, 'the pretty one'. She never left the garden, but Bilbo watched out for her and kept her safe.

Well, the kittens became cats and I remember taking Bilbo in for a booster jab at the vet's. As they did the usual check-up the vet told me then that Bilbo had a heart murmur. There was nothing really to be done and I was told that cats can live their whole lives with a murmur, and I shouldn't be too concerned. I guess it was at this point, though, that I realised just how much Bilbo had come to mean to me – there was a flash of reality and indeed a sudden awareness of his mortality – but we went home and he went about his business without a care in the world and so did I.

So, another eight years on and I remember one Saturday afternoon Bilbo had come back home after an adventure and didn't have the usual spring in his step. While I could see no visible signs of injury, I thought perhaps he had perhaps had a scare or misjudged a jump. The following day he showed little sign of improvement and I resolved to take him to the vet's on Monday.

On Sunday evening he wasn't moving well at all and so we decided to take him in that evening to see the emergency vet. They were pretty sure that it was a blood clot preventing the flow of blood to his back legs and said they could try and inject him with something to help but that there was always a chance that another clot could come. We both wanted them to try and so they kept him in and on Monday they called and said he was much the same. I wanted to visit him and so on Monday evening we went to see him, and they said if there hadn't been much improvement by the next day then we needed to consider what to do next.

I remember lying in bed that Monday night next to my wife and not hearing his oh-so-familiar purr in my ear, and knowing he was alone and so were we. Although we lay together that night, we both felt so desperately alone without Bilbo. We prayed and we wept, and it felt like dawn would never come – we wanted it to and yet we didn't.

Daybreak came and I rang the vet with Helen standing right by my side. I expected the worse, in fact I was already thinking of how to comfort Helen, but the news was good. He had perked up and eaten something that morning and seemed to be a little better. They told us if he continued to improve, we could go and pick him up that evening, and so we did.

Even the vet seemed amazed at his improvement when we collected him. We took him home and for that next week he recovered his strength, and he refound his feet and was back out in the garden, just like his old self again. I truly treasured that week, it was like a gift from God, he lay on me each night. It felt like a miracle.

Then the morning came when I went downstairs to find him on our kitchen floor with his legs completely gone and him dragging himself along by his front feet. It was terrible to see – even remembering it now will always haunt me. I knew then his time with us was up. The vet confirmed my fears; not one but two or three large clots. There was nothing more to be done.

We went together to the vet's to put him to sleep, I stroked his head and brushed my thumb over his face and called him by name as the drug was administered. I knew it was the right thing to do.

We left the vet's bleary-eyed, eyes full of tears. On my way out I remember thanking the receptionist for all their care and was aware that she too started to weep as I left. It occurred to me that they dealt with this all the time, but perhaps there are some things you don't get used to.

I don't recall crying in public like that before; we sat for 20 minutes in the car and fixed our faces and then we drove to a local beauty spot and looked out at the sea. We didn't say much to each other. The time just seemed to stop passing. Eventually I turned to Helen and said, 'Come on, let's go home.'

The coming days were a rollercoaster of emotion. Sharing the news with others. Finding his cat hair in places he used to sleep and hide. The strangest of things would set me off crying, and then I would set Helen off. I often told myself: 'You're being ridiculous'; 'He was just a cat'; 'He wasn't a friend or a relative, it shouldn't be affecting you like this'; 'Pull yourself together and man up'. After speaking with close friends, though, it really helped me to realise that this advice I told myself was just bad advice. Grief forges its own path it seems, and it is different for each of us. It's better to ride out the waves rather than stand up to the tide like Canute did. The talking really helped.

Helen was amazing. She gave me a new photo of Bilbo for my bedside and she made a large framed collage of photos of us with him, which we hung up on the wall. I was so thankful for these and they remain treasured to this day. I feel like we celebrated him and honoured him with these and that was important to us.

It's been nearly three years now since his passing. Ginny (who had always deferred to Bilbo) after a week or two found her voice and suddenly became a lot bolder, it was as if Bilbo had left some of his indomitable spirit in her. She would never even enter our bedroom while Bilbo was alive – that was 'Bilbo's room' as far as she was concerned, I remember she used to run straight back out if you ever took her in there. A couple of weeks after Bilbo died, I woke up in the middle of the night to find her on our bed sleeping on my back, purring away, just like Bilbo used to. I remember almost doing a double-take as I craned my head round to look. I cried silently as I went back to sleep, being careful not to disturb her. It was as if, somehow, she knew what I needed.

Cats are remarkable, really. When you own a cat it's you that serves them most of the time and yet, somehow, they know what you need before you even do. Ginny has thrived over the last three years since Bilbo's passing and is still with us to this day, pretending she is old, hobbling up the steps and then running like the clappers round the garden when she thinks we are not looking. She has become quite the character. People often ask me if we will ever get any more cats and, you know, I honestly don't know the answer. It feels like a question for another time.

The grief gradually eased around Bilbo as time went on. We would find old photos or a toy behind a piece of furniture and we would get little pangs of grief, but we did find a way forward. We will always love and remember him.

What to Say

Remember, showing up is ultimately what matters. Don't be so afraid of saying the wrong thing that you hide away and say nothing at all. I would much rather have someone say something – even if they occasionally put their foot in it – than someone who ignores my suffering.

Let the bereaved set the tone and the agenda rather than presuming. Let them say if they feel happy, sad, confused or lost. If they control the dialogue, it ensures what you say is appropriate to how they feel in that moment.

Ask in-depth questions, not just surface ones

It is easy to stick to 'safe' questions: for example, 'How are you doing today?' However, most of the time people will have become so practised at answering these that they answer before they even think, and will reply, 'Coping, thanks,' or, 'I'm okay, thanks.' By just going a little broader and reframing questions, you can properly engage with people who need to talk about their pain.

How about asking:

* 'What was your most difficult moment to navigate this week?'
* 'Did you find joy in anything this week?'
* 'Was there anything you needed this week that I could have helped you with?'

Pay close attention to their response. If they respond openly, that's great. If they don't, spend time thinking about how better to phrase a question the next time you see them. Prior preparation can make you feel more confident in your interaction, and once you have truly engaged them in conversation, you won't need to say much as the bereaved person will do most of the talking.

Ask questions about their experience of loss

People are often desperate to share their stories (even if they do shed copious amounts of tears in the process). Of course, some of these may be hard to hear, but some will also be beautiful.

Every time you sit and listen to a bereaved person's story, you are giving them a real gift. You are also showing them that their loss, their beloved pet, was worthy of your time and attention.

> 'Sometimes, only one person is missing, and the whole world seems depopulated.'
>
> Alphonse de Lamartine

Korver

Our journey to have a longed-for baby tragically ended in a miscarriage. My husband and I desperately wanted to have a child to love and to cherish, but infertility took a toll on us. Three years into our marriage we finally decided to get a pet dog, and we named him Korver. The moment Korver took his first paw-step in our home our lives were changed forever.

We didn't treat Korver like a pet, he was more like a baby to us, and our world revolved around him. Negative pregnancy results keep coming and it was a hard pill to swallow. One day I came home after another negative test result weeping in despair, but suddenly my boy Korver came to me and licked my tears and it felt like he was assuring me that everything would be okay. He calmed my emotions and he kept doing that over the years.

Then, one beautiful afternoon we were overjoyed to finally get a positive test result. When we were least expecting it, those two lines shone bright – I was pregnant! We were so excited for the future and couldn't wait to see Korver and our baby together.

Our little girl Nissha finally arrived, after five years of waiting for a child to hold. However, she didn't survive for long – she lived for only 52 days, and then we lost her. She was gone forever, her life extinguished before it even properly began.

I was depressed and on the floor, broken with grief, but through it all my Korver was a source of comfort. He helped me live in the midst of despair. I'm not even sure if I would have survived those dark days without him.

A year later we were surprised once again with good news – I was pregnant once again. On the day that I was due to deliver the baby I kissed Korver and told him to wait for me as I would soon be home with a newborn baby sister.

Three days later I was discharged from the hospital and with great excitement I took my baby home. I went straight in the house to find Korver to introduce him to our daughter. I called his name but he didn't respond, and I felt a strange feeling of fear that is hard to explain. I ran towards him in his bed and found him no longer breathing. I was beyond shocked and I couldn't process the emotions I was engulfed by.

For years Korver and I had been together, we had shared laughter and sorrow, and in the blink of an eye he was gone. He was the source of my comfort and joy. He knew when I was up and when I was down. He gave me a reason to wake up each day and even when I didn't want to move from my bed, I did for him, as his life depended on me.

Life felt so unfair. Through losing babies and facing infertility he was there, and when that longed-for moment arrived for me to introduce my daughter to Korver he was gone. My heart still aches for him every single day.

People around me couldn't understand why I grieved so much for a dog. To them he was just a pet, but to me he was part of our family, he was my four-legged child.

Korver took a piece of my heart with him and my life will never be the same again without him. Thank you, Korver, for everything, thank you for making us happy, thank you for filling the empty spaces in our hearts, thank you for dedicating your life to us.

What to Do

Most people will rush to support friends who are grieving a person in the couple of weeks immediately following a loss, however people rarely offer care to those who have lost pets. Perhaps people deem the loss as being less significant than that of a person (and of course it is different), but pets are family members.

For some people, and for all sorts of reasons, the loss of a pet can be every bit as traumatic as the death of a human: an animal may be the only companion for someone; perhaps a pet has journeyed with someone through traumatic times; or maybe a couple can't have children and their four-legged friend has filled that void. Whatever the case may be, if someone is heartbroken after the loss of their pet they need and deserve compassionate, long-lasting support.

How you can help:

Ensure they have details of the support available to them

People have to want support, and reaching out for it is the first part of their healing process.

Do things that show the bereaved person you are thinking of them

Even if you can't see them face to face, you can send them notes, text messages, cards, gifts. A book can be a helpful gift so that, if and when they feel they need help or assistance, it will already be at their fingertips.

Make a note in your diary of key anniversaries

If you feel it is appropriate you might reach out to the bereaved in the weeks before the date to say, 'I am thinking of you, leading up to the anniversary of such-and-such an event' – this means the world to grieving people. Then also reach out to them on the day, even if you only send a card. And try to remember to contact them a few weeks after and ask them how they coped.

Offer practical help at home

Try to be more specific than saying, 'Call me if you need help.' Instead try: 'Are you okay with me bringing dinner over next week?' Or, 'Can I stock your freezer with a few ready-made meals so that there is food there if you don't fancy cooking?' Or, 'Can I come and clean the house with you, as I am sure it is hard being in the house right now?'

When someone is struggling to survive the weight of grief, household chores are the last thing on their mind, and if you can help make their living environment a nicer or tidier space, that is a gift. When you spend a lot of time crying on the bathroom floor, it being clean is a blessing.

Childcare

If the bereaved person has children, offer to help take care of them. While it is good for children to see that grief and loss are part of life, and that crying is okay and indeed healthy, they also have a limit on how much they can tolerate. If you can take them out and allow them to have times of fun and joy amid the sorrow, that can be helpful.

Offer physical comfort (if appropriate)

Now, this comes with a warning, as some people hate physical touch and will avoid it at all costs. Not everyone's a hugger, so only make physical contact if you know the person well enough to be sure they will welcome it.

Touch is important when offering compassion and empathy because it can make people feel heard and loved. Just holding their hand or hugging them can make them feel safer, grounded and cared for.

Arrange meetings/hang-outs where they will feel at ease being themselves

Many people aren't naturally comfortable at formal events like dinner parties at the best of times, and such things are even harder when you feel bereft, so try to create more casual and relaxed opportunities, so they don't feel a need to put on a 'brave face'. Please also be mindful of holding events and not inviting the bereaved person, as that can cause real hurt. So, yes, you may need to change how you do things for a few weeks or months, but if it helps the grieving person, surely it's worth it?

Be flexible with plans

Make it clear you are fine if arrangements change right up to the last minute. Often what stops people who are grieving making plans is that they are worried they may suddenly not feel able to go out, which means it feels safer to them not to make any arrangements with anyone for fear of letting others down. By giving them permission always to change, cancel or move events, you will provide them with the peace of mind they need to take the risk.

If/when the person does change arrangements, be sure to never make them feel guilty or to look put out (even if you have to do a fantastic acting job).

Be forgiving and patient

When journeying through grief, it can mean a person feels so overwhelmed and numb that they stop being thoughtful or kind. They may appear either emotionless or too emotional. They may be brutal in their responses and lack sensitivity in how they phrase things. They may not think to ask how your day went or for news on your work promotion. Remember, this isn't personal, and it does not mean the bereaved person has become selfish and self-centred. It just says they are trying to navigate life right now, and they are so overwhelmed with pain that their typical responses to things are on hold. Give them time, and they will start asking about you again; it won't always be about them.

'Not the least hard thing to bear when they go from us, these quiet friends, is that they carry away with them so many years of our own lives.'

John Galsworthy

Roscoe

Five years have passed since I lost my best friend. He was my most loyal companion and by my side for 20 years, supporting me through many life experiences. He made me laugh and smile during the hard times and made the good times even more rewarding. On 7 July 2016 I lost my best friend. I still think of him and miss him every single day. That day was one of the worst days of my life and I still go through each moment wondering if there was something more that I could have done to save him.

His name was Roscoe and he was the most handsome, wonderful Pomeranian I had ever seen. He had a smile that would blow anyone away and the most loving eyes you could ever imagine. I will never forget the day when this little angel came into my life so very unexpectedly.

I was in my early twenties and it was a dark time for me. I was going through a lot at the time. My parents had just divorced, my family was gone and I was completely devastated. I had also just got out of a rough relationship and I felt like I had no one to turn to or confide in. It was a very lonely time in my life. I was scared and had no idea how I was going to recover from that. I remember crying myself to sleep numerous times because I felt so frightened and alone.

One morning I got up and decided to take myself shopping for a new winter coat. As I started walking through the mall, I walked past a pet store. I turned my head and saw this beautiful little ball of orange fur. Immediately I had to go in and ask the assistant if I could hold him. It was almost as if fate was pulling me into that store. Waiting for the assistant to bring him to the meeting area was the longest three minutes of my life. I was so excited to meet this adorable pup. The first thing I noticed when she opened up the gate was his eyes. They were the brightest, shiniest eyes I had ever seen. He looked so playful and his tail was wagging a mile a minute. I hadn't even held him yet and he already had my heart. We played for a little while, and he rolled over on his back and asked me to pet his belly. He played tug-of-war with my shoelaces and then he invited himself up on my lap, putting his head on my shoulder. That was it for me. I ended up going home with a puppy that day. I had to go back for the coat another day, but I didn't mind. I had a new best friend.

Everything finally started to change when I brought him home. I was happier. This dog that I named Roscoe lifted my spirits from day one and continued to do that for 20 years. We had a very long, adventurous, playful life together. We always took road trips, went for the longest walks, he even helped me clean up the kitchen floor by eating whatever table scraps 'fell' from my plate. If I was having a bad day, all he wanted to do was cuddle. If I wasn't feeling well, he'd rest his head on my chest and give me kisses. When I had a great day, he celebrated with me. Fetch was his favourite sport. He mastered the game and even had me chasing after the ball when he would 'throw' it back to me.

I was very blessed to have Roscoe by my side for so many years. He made me feel complete, he made me happy and he loved me no matter what was going on in my life at any time. That unconditional love is priceless. I no longer felt alone or scared, I had my best friend. He was my family. Our bond was a very special one and I know he felt it too. He was very loyal and loving throughout his entire life. He came into my life when I needed him the most and I am very grateful for that. Twenty years is a long time, much longer than Pomeranians usually live for, but now it feels like it wasn't enough.

Roscoe was diagnosed with stomach cancer during the last year of his life. I kept him as comfortable as I could and made sure that he was not suffering. He remained playful most of the time but sometimes he just wanted to sleep because he was tired. He had lumps behind his legs, which made it difficult for him to walk and sometimes to even stand. I tried to mentally prepare myself for what was coming but it was a struggle. How do you say goodbye to your best friend? I didn't know what I would do without him. I was scared again, but I loved him enough to not want him to suffer. Roscoe gave me 20 wonderful years and remained loyal and loving throughout, I had to do the same for him.

He began to show me the signs that he was ready. He was tired. He stopped eating and I knew I had to make the hardest decision of my life. The day of his appointment, we spent the entire afternoon together. We cuddled, I gave him a nice gentle bath, and I thanked him for being a part of my life. I stayed by his side that whole afternoon until he was asleep and heading to the rainbow bridge. I asked him to wait for me and I know he will. The days that followed were sad and long. I cried for days and I still cry at times. A lot of times, actually. I think of things that I could have or should have done differently. I find myself still looking for him on certain spots of the couch where he used to lounge. I still have all of his toys in a box and I don't think I'll ever part with them. Some people think that it's easier to get over the loss of a pet than a person but I disagree. I've been grieving and missing him for a long time and I think I always will. He was very special to me and was one of the biggest parts of my life, it's not easy to get over that or to replace that.

I try to focus on the good things, on the fact that I got to spend 20 years with him. That I gave him a nice life. That I have so many wonderful memories of him. I will cherish those memories forever. When I get sad about losing him, I think of the silly things he used to do when he knew I needed cheering up, and it still works. He's still with me, alive in my heart and my memories. I am very grateful for that. One of my friends tried to console me when he passed away by saying that I did a good thing by rescuing him from the pet store and giving him a good life. I agree with some of that, but I didn't rescue Roscoe. Roscoe rescued me.

4

Healing and the Quest
For Happiness

In the aftermath of loss it can feel almost impossible to imagine feeling happy again. We might doubt that we can ever heal from the pain, but I want to reassure you that it won't feel this overwhelming forever. I also feel it's important to stress that one can't rush the grieving process and, by trying to, you risk slowing the process down still further. So take it one day at a time and give yourself the time and grace to heal.

Two of the questions I am asked most often are 'How can you heal after loss?' and 'How can I feel happy again?' Every situation is different, but in my work I have noticed some similarities in the emotions experienced around pet loss, and I share those with you here in the hope it helps you navigate this complex time.

Healing

'Do people heal post-loss?' is a question I am constantly asked, and sadly it is one of the hardest questions to answer. In a nutshell, the answer is that some do, and some don't.

My personal experience of pet loss might help to explain how complex this subject is.

First of all, I guess we need to decipher what is meant by 'heal'. To me, *not* healing means someone feels:

* Despair
* Hopelessness
* In physical and mental torture about the loss
* Constantly unhappy

I don't feel those things any more, which is why I consider my heart to have healed. I fully accept I have had pets who have died, and I have come to terms with the pain of losing them. I will always be sad that they aren't now with me, but I also feel blessed that they were here at all.

But that doesn't mean I act as though they never existed.

Will I always talk about them?

YES, they were a wonderful part of my family and my life.

Do I miss them?

Yes.

Do I wish they hadn't died?

Yes, of course!

Do I have times where grief can hit me out of nowhere?

Yes! Very, very rarely, but I still have those times.

So why do some people not heal following the loss of a pet? This is almost impossible to answer definitively, as everyone is unique, but I think I can unravel some of the myths surrounding it.

If someone doesn't heal, does it mean they must have loved their pet more than someone else whose heart has healed?

No, of course it doesn't. Love and healing aren't linked.

Can we make people heal?

No, we can't. Everyone's walk is unique to them: some start on the path a day after a loss; for others it's months; for some it may take years; and for others, sadly, it never happens. When my heart started to mend after we had lost Jake, I knew it would be a very different shape from what it had been before, and that was okay. In fact, that was better, as I wanted loss to have changed me. My heart was now bigger than ever, because the love for my wonderful boy had expanded its capacity, so a new shape was a good thing.

Are there obstacles that can make healing harder for some people?

Yes, there are, in particular:

* **Personality:** How we journey through loss and life in general can be shaped by our personality and character traits.
* **Upbringing:** How we are raised, and the skills we have developed through life experiences, definitely play a part in how we recover from trauma and loss.
* **Lack of joy:** If a person's life has no hope within it, or they have nothing to look forward to in the future, recovery from trauma and loss is more challenging.

In summary

I was broken-hearted; my heart was rebuilt in a different shape from before.

But I kept talking about the loss and my experiences – talking is key to the brain and heart accepting what has happened, and it helps any trauma connected to the loss to be processed.

I have shared my story of pet loss so publicly to try to bring hope to people who are desperate, to show that pet loss grief is as valid as any other form of grief. I also want people to know that it is possible to be happy again after loss. Sometimes you just need to hear someone say that.

Having a healed heart does not mean that people won't at times feel broken, or feel acute pain, or feel grief-stricken and freshly bereaved. This is part of a grief journey; the path is littered with twists and turns.

'The dog is the most faithful of animals and would be much esteemed were it not so common. Our Lord God has made his greatest gift the commonest.'

Martin Luther

Sophie

Her name was Sophie, a golden retriever, 10 years old. This girl came into my life when I needed her the most. She was a pure breed that someone didn't want any more, and the best 150 bucks I have ever spent.

She became my rock and my safe space.

I went through domestic violence a few years back, became a single mum with two growing boys while progressing in my job. It's been really hard finding myself, accepting I'm not to blame, but at the end of a hard day she was there. She knew, she always did. I called her my shadow.

I brought her to work every day (I work in a pet retail store). Customers and staff loved her, she just had this calming effect on everyone. Whether it was me or a team member having a bad day, she stuck to them like glue in case they needed her. She picked up on my anxiety all the time; the girls would watch her on the security cameras as I was unaware that from a distance that she had my back.

Three months ago, I brought her to work like any other day; she was happy and healthy, running around with the zoomics as she was just so excited to be there.

All of a sudden, she stopped. The offering of treats was refused, which in her language meant something was seriously wrong. She collapsed and the girls came running out to me screaming, 'Something's wrong with Soph!' I have never run so fast in my life!

We scooped up 36kg of golden fluff and carried her to my car. One of my girls came with me to keep her calm, because I was far from calm. My partner met us at the vet, where Sophie's stomach blew out rapidly. They couldn't figure out what it was but they knew she had a build-up of fluid. We transferred her to an emergency vet for an ultrasound specialist, and it took him five minutes to diagnose her with a ruptured spleen. It had been slowly growing silently for a while and she was filling with blood. She looked at me as if to say, 'Mum, I'm tired now.'

I was devastated. This girl was my world. 'She has been through everything with me,' I thought, 'it can't be her time to go, everyone at work will be upset – they love her too!' I thought I must have been dreaming. It was only three hours ago she was doing zoomies at work and munching on treats customers bought her.

As I said my goodbyes, I thanked her for getting me through the hardest time in my life. I promised her she would always be remembered and loved.

There was an expected emptiness at home and breaking the news to my boys was extremely difficult. I had a week off work, because working at a pet store would be possibly the worst place I could go. Even after I came back the shop felt empty without her. My girls were beyond supportive and every time a golden retriever came in one of them would rush out to get me.

I honestly felt like a part of me had died.

The funny thing was, I think she knew I was going to be okay. She knew her job was done and now my partner was here she could leave. I had been through hell with her by my side, but now that I'm literally the happiest and the most content I have ever been she could retire because someone else finally had my back.

Three months on I still miss her like crazy and the pain is still there, I just manage it better. It gets easier to live without her now she is rested and back with us in a memorial piece I had done. She hangs on my wall looking over me and my boys.

Many of my team had a special bond with her so, as much as I was grieving, they were too. I organised a little lock of her fur in a frame for two girls in particular.

It feels unfair that I didn't get time with Sophie after her diagnosis and that it happened so fast, but words cannot express how proud I was to have been her human and how she touched the souls of everyone she met.

Until we meet again, my sweet girl.

The Quest for Happiness – My Story

After Jake died, I spent endless nights wailing on the floor, repeating over and over, 'I just want to be happy again – someone tell me how to be happy.' I had gone through so much significant loss, I couldn't understand how losing our wonderful dog was the thing that utterly broke me. It truly felt like the final nail in my coffin.

Losing my sense of happiness was probably a major layer of my grief. I had always considered myself a truly happy, joy-filled person, and to have this part of me suddenly removed felt like I had lost my identity. I didn't recognise this sad, heartbroken person staring back at me in the mirror. The eyes that used to shine with expectation and excitement now looked lifeless and terrified – who was I without a smile on my face?

I guess this is when my quest to discover what happiness truly meant began. Maybe true happiness could still be found following heartbreak and loss; maybe, just maybe, I could still be happy, even in the depths of grief – perhaps one can be in mourning and still be a happy person?

So, what did this quest look like in practical terms? I started by acknowledging all the beautiful things I still had in my life. I won't bore you with listing them here, as your list would be unique to you and comparison helps no one. But we all have something to be grateful for. Perhaps it is your partner, your soul mate; maybe it's having lots of friends to support you, or one special friend who has been able to carry you through tragedy. Whatever or whoever you include on your list, just by taking time to consider how blessed you are to have them in your life can tweak your perspective – it definitely changed mine.

I chose not to say, 'Why?' Instead I said, 'Why not?' This stopped me feeling victimised by life, and made me face the fact that these terrible things happen to many people (too many people), and I wasn't being singled out. It wasn't because I deserved it, or that life was picking on me – it's simply the nature of loss and grief; it doesn't discriminate, it targets anyone and everyone.

I decided to let go of the deep desperation to feel happy again – the more I talked about the loss of my joy and the more I dissected why I couldn't be happy again, the sadder I felt. I had to choose to let it go, and say, 'If I am never happy again, then that is okay. Is it what I desired? No. Would I like it to be different? Yes. But longing for it doesn't bring it back.'

Next, I decided to read about people who had overcome tragedy. I soaked up every story I could find about those who had been broken by life, but had somehow kept going. This stopped me feeling sorry for myself and made me look in awe at these amazing people who are dotted around the globe. People who you would think should be rocking in a corner, but who are instead leading meaningful lives. I saw how loss had transformed their souls – and I made a choice to be one of these people.

That didn't mean I needed to do something extraordinary, it just meant I wasn't going to let loss destroy my future; I was going to find hope in the darkness. I noticed that none of these beautiful humans talked much about happiness – happiness was a small emotion compared to what they were feeling and expressing.

Anything can make you happy, and happiness is a transient state and emotion. Being fulfilled, compassionate, empathetic and a good human are all way more important.

I said to my husband that we needed to do something for people who are desperate and unhappy right now. It didn't matter what it was, but I needed to know that what we did would help someone feel cared for. We chose to make hampers for people who were alone and lonely, massive hampers that would feed them for weeks. It was a big task and took us weeks to do – but boy, did it feel good to know people wouldn't be going hungry, and also would feel loved.

Then we put together rucksacks for people who were homeless – these included sleeping bags, socks, wet wipes, mints, notepads and pens, tissues, toothbrushes and so much more. We then handed them to groups working with homeless people across two cities. Again, this took us weeks – but we felt like we were doing something to help other people and I can't tell you how good that felt.

These are just two of the many things we did, and I can wholeheartedly recommend you do something that removes you from your own pain for a short amount of time, and makes you look at the wider world.

Two words of caution here. Firstly, please don't volunteer for things and not follow through; charities have so few resources and when people let them down it really affects them. Secondly, don't offer to do anything that means you need to provide emotional support – wait until your heart has mended to do that.

A massive milestone then happened: I gave myself permission to feel joy again. I realised that me smiling didn't mean I wasn't grieving any more for our precious boy Jake. So, I watched as much stand-up comedy as I could. I watched Nigella cooking delicious food, Oprah conducting inspiring interviews and *The Vicar of Dibley* on repeat on TV. If it was going to make me laugh or smile, or bring me any enjoyment, I said, 'Yes, please, bring it on.'

I then wrote down how I was feeling, in notepads, journals, anywhere I could find space to express my feelings. Pain needs a voice at times, and if we can let it flow out of us in words, it can help the brain accept the circumstances we now live in.

Next, I realised I had been delaying my happiness with thoughts such as: 'If x happens, I will feel happy again. If y and z happen, I will find my peace.' I decided it was time to stop postponing things and making excuses for why I couldn't feel it. I could feel happy right now if I chose to – even in the depths of my darkness. I could be a happy person and a broken person simultaneously.

Over time, it then happened. Not in a way I imagined it would. I wanted to be as happy as I was prior to going through loss and grief, but to my surprise I was now happier than I had been before.

Life had more meaning. The depth of pain I experienced had created new, much deeper reserves in my soul. Those reserves could be filled with joy, and as they were now way deeper they could hold so much more happiness.

I can't promise you this is a foolproof way to rediscover happiness; all I can say is that this is how I found mine again. If any of this helps lead you to the path to find your smile, I will be delighted.

'Heaven goes by favor. If it went by merit, you would stay out and your dog would go in.'

Mark Twain

Holly

I picked up Holly as a tiny kitten, from a house in a big estate.

Holly was the smallest of the litter, and she was so resilient. She was a 'converter'. People who didn't like cats, she'd seek them out and turn them into cat lovers! Her tiny face, soft fur and glistening eyes were spellbinding.

She adored the man who is now my husband the first time she met him. That's how I knew he was the one.

In 2018, I was pregnant with our first child. Holly lay on my belly every night, showing her horror that there was movement under her once comfortable seat.

Our son sadly passed away before he could come home from hospital, in March 2019. I hit a place lower than rock bottom. I wanted to be dead with my son. Through everything, Holly sat on my belly every day. She was my constant. If it wasn't for her, I might have done something stupid. With her by my side, how could I leave? She would never understand where I'd gone. She would never know why.

We had our rainbow baby in February 2021. While pregnant, Holly took up her throne once more, atop my growing bump, again showing her displeasure at this little life wriggling within me. When our baby came home,

Holly would just pop in and out of the room we were in but would rush over to the baby when she cried. When she settled, Holly would either lie down or go to another room again.

We finally took Holly to the vet's because she had been steadily losing weight since Christmas. The pandemic made it difficult to get her seen, but she wasn't in any obvious discomfort.

Her tiny frame made the weight loss so obvious. The vet weighed her and told us she had lost a third of her bodyweight since her last check-up, and we needed to know why. Blood tests confirmed she had hyperthyroidism. It also highlighted that the heart murmur she'd had from birth had significantly worsened. She was put on medication and it really seemed to start to help her. We were aware of her advancing age, and we just wanted to do what was best for her.

On 19 June 2021, Holly went for her last sleep. She had gone for a nap behind a neighbour's shed, and just didn't wake up.

I forget she's not here sometimes. I start to call her, but stop myself. It catches in my throat, and a pain in my heart sometimes stops me in my tracks. Now she won't come running over if I call her. I cry sometimes just because I miss her. I'm not ashamed! She's still mine. She's still my little furry family member, it's just she's no longer on this earthly plane.

I had over 12 years of love and adoration with my sweet girl. She kept me going when I feared my life was over. I like to think that she came to me at the right time in my life, and stayed until she knew I was okay.

Every single one of Holly's nine lives were a gift. From the first one where she jumped onto my plate of piping-hot lasagne as a kitten, to her last one where she just went for a nice nap.

I always promised her that I'd never leave her. I have her ashes in a beautiful box in the living room, in the corner where she sat and supervised our day-to-day routines. When my time comes, we'll be scattered together. As I always said to her, 'Me and you, Holls, against the world. I'll never leave you.' And that will always be true.

I remember her so fondly, and I still cannot believe that she's really no longer here. She will never know how much I truly loved and appreciated her companionship, love and joy. My loyal friend. I'm so glad she was mine and I was hers.

I miss my Holly so much.

APPENDIX 1

Ten Questions About Grief

I am always amazed at the diverse questions that I get asked at events and on social media, and I thought it might be helpful to include some of the most asked here:

1. What personally shocked you about grief?

Many, many things. I may have trained as a counsellor prior to experiencing loss, but nothing in the world could have prepared me for walking the path I did.

One thing that surprised me was that my heart wasn't just broken because of the losses (of people and pets); my heart also broke due to the mammoth disappointment I was carrying, and due to the terror of the unknown. The agony was kind of surreal, and it made me feel like I had left the planet and had transcended to a different universe.

I was shocked at the million questions that rushed around my brain. 'What if you don't survive this?' 'What if you are sad forever?' 'What if you never stop crying?' Oh, the questions, the never-ending questions of a brain that seems to seek to destroy you when you are deeply broken.

I found the only way to survive this was not to torture myself with seeking the answers; I simply kept telling myself the same thing on repeat: 'I will survive this.' I gave in to the pain, I submitted to the questions that only grief born from deep love can pose and, over time, the questions stopped – but nothing could have prepared me for this part of grief.

I was so shocked at the immense fear I experienced. Grief really does throw you into a huge black pit. C.S. Lewis said, 'Nothing prepared me for the fact that grief looks so like fear.' And boy, does that quote ring true. Grief does look so like terror; it is daunting and all-consuming. I feared everything. I feared waking up each morning as I knew I would have to live through another day of fresh pain. I feared going to sleep because of the nightmares. Often when you have a bad dream you wake up and reassure yourself that it is just a dream and nothing to be scared of, but during that time I would wake up and realise the night-mare was real, it was true life – and that really terrified me.

The most shocking thing, I suppose, was that the black-est grief, the haunting, harrowing, please-kill-me-now type of grief, did end. For a long time I didn't think it would, but it did. It gradually changed and became less and less. I would no longer say I am mourning. While I am fully aware grief is a lifelong passage, I don't feel broken any longer. In fact, I feel more whole than I have ever been, and happier than ever – I never believed that was possible in the aftermath of loss. When you are processing grief you are building your grief muscles, so even though the loss doesn't reduce in size and weight, you personally get stronger, so carrying it stops consuming you.

2. What was the worst part of pet loss for you?

I think one of the worst parts was feeling like the pain was infinite. There was no end in sight, and that is a truly hard thing to live with. The most harrowing part of loss was knowing that however long I waited and however many tears I wept, my pets were never coming back.

Over time I was able to accept that, while their physical presence here with me was limited, the love I carried for them was never-ending, and that meant they will always be here with me, and that helped ease the pain.

3. Where did you find strength to go on?

My strength came when I said, 'I will no longer run from this pain.' I faced the battle; with shaking legs and a quivering lip, I said, 'I will not hide from the agony, I will process it.' Even if that meant wailing on the floor in a pool of tears.

To be expected to face another day on this planet while carrying the weight of grief on your shoulders can be daunting. And to find any kind of strength when you feel broken is pretty impossible, so I tell everyone not to even look for it. Your only task is to take one step forwards today; you don't need to find any hidden reserve – strength will find you, if you don't find it. Whether it finds you in that pool of tears in the valley, or while you are walking on a mountain top – wherever you may be, it will sneak up on you, I promise you.

4. How did you feel ready to move on with life and get another pet?

If I always waited until I felt mentally or emotionally ready for things, I would do nothing. My secret? I show up, however I feel.

I also decided to learn from everything – to constantly look for a hidden lesson, or a gift or a blessing, even in the deepest of traumas (which, believe me, isn't easy). I can say, hand-on-heart, that this was a big game-changer for me, as it made me look more positively at things.

In terms of being ready to have another pet in our family, that was a hard decision. I wondered if it was the right thing for us, and I wondered whether having another dog was asking for more pain in our lives. The bottom line is, having another pet brought us so much joy. If we make all life choices based on the chance of experiencing pain down the line we would be robbing ourselves and our families of countless blessings.

5. What do you most wish someone had told you when you were going through grief?

Grief can make you hide in the shadows, but it helps to lean into the light

I was so scared to show the real me, the broken me, and it often felt easier to hide that pain away, especially when it came to losing our pets, as I was afraid I would be judged by people. But if we courageously choose to be vulnerable and let the light hit our faces, we can crawl through the valley of darkness much more easily. Often, we find others who are also crawling, and these people can become lifelong friends – I call them 'valley friends'. They have followed the same path, and they are usually the people who understand you the most.

The pain is not limited, as the love is endless

Knowing this would have helped me understand and accept the pain I was going through.

You don't need to fight to survive

I often used to scream that I couldn't make it through another day, and I didn't want to live a moment longer with the raw agony that only loss can bring. After some time, I discovered I didn't need to fight the pain; the only thing I needed to do was open my eyes when I woke up and bravely look at the heartbreak and refuse to run from it. To have been told this would have helped me a lot.

There will be days when you are hit by a fresh wave of grief

And on those days you will doubt how far you have swum in the ocean of mourning. Let me reassure you that these waves are part of the journey, they won't pull you back to the beginning. In fact, they do the exact opposite; they carry you forwards if you don't fight them – just hold on to your lifebelt and let the current carry you on. You won't drown, and you may need to tell yourself this a hundred times a day. Let it become your mantra: 'I won't drown; I am just learning to swim.'

When walking through grief, feelings change by the hour

Heck, let's be even more realistic, they can change by the second. So, if someone asks you if you are okay now, that doesn't mean you need to be okay in 60 minutes, or that you were okay yesterday. Just try to stay as present as you can.

Grief isn't something you can control

I think a huge misconception about grief is that it is control-lable, that people can choose when and where to feel it and process it – before going through loss I probably believed this a little too, if I'm honest. Once you have experienced grief first-hand you can only laugh at this myth. Can you control love? No, of course you can't; love is a powerful force that controls people. Well, the same applies to grief, and we must respect that. Knowing this would have helped me no end.

Sometimes all the explaining in the world won't help others understand loss and grief

This is especially true if you are explaining your grief (con-nected to losing your pet) to a non-animal lover. People will always view things from their own level of perception and from their own personal experience.

6. Did grief bring you any gifts?

Grief made me rip up the rule book. Suddenly, I got to just be me. I stopped wanting to conform and please those around me. Maybe I was beyond caring? Perhaps I was so broken I felt no shame in sobbing on the floor? Whatever the case, it brought me a freedom to be truly authentic and that really is a gift.

My pets lost of all their tomorrows, but because of them I embrace all of my todays – that is a gift.

It's in the brokenness . . .

It's in the waiting . . .

It's in the pain . . .

It's in the darkest of places . . .

. . . that we discover the depth of the love we are able to feel.

That is a gift.

7. Why does grief make people feel out of control?

We all like to control our destiny and there is nothing more out of our control than grief. It's not possible for us to predict or defer death, and as such we can't stop grief from entering our lives. Grief brings with it chaos. It collects every element of our lives, puts it all into a big basket and then shakes it.

Things may break in that basket, things will certainly change shape, and the pieces will always come out in a strange and confusing order. No part of this is easy to bear.

Many assume grief needs to be conquered, but actually it is something people need to face and not fight. This takes a real leap of faith and a complete release of control. It takes real trust to let it surround you like fog on a mountain top, but eventually a path will open up before you and you can move forwards.

8. What would you say to someone who is trying to stop a family member or friend from crying?

When you see someone crying, please remember that tears have a voice. That voice is so rarely listened to; it is mostly ignored and told to stay quiet for fear of inducing more weeping. But something magical happens if we listen. Those droplets of water speak the profound truth and tell life-changing stories – so listen to those teardrops. And bear the following in mind:

* To have someone there to catch every tear is a beautiful gift – you can give that gift to a bereaved person.
* It's easy to sit on the shoreline and judge those swimming in the ocean of grief. Never say, 'Perhaps you should stop crying.'
* You might think it will help to try to look for a bright side even in tragedy. But sometimes there isn't a bright side, however much people want there to be. Sometimes it's just crap. Agonisingly painful. Overwhelmingly terrible – and we just have to accept that, and give people the freedom to sob.

9. What do you want people to know about people who are grieving?

Bereaved people frequently feel pressured not to talk of the pet they have lost, because society wants to avoid mentioning them by name. It's as if the bereaved are being forced to rip out the pages of their life story where their pets once resided. But the bereaved usually want their pets to be celebrated. You can help this happen by talking about these beautiful companions and by not fearing the subject of loss.

Be aware that it is pretty hard to articulate the pain. Most people are taught the language to express joy, but there are rarely lessons in how to communicate devastating loss. I had no clue how to express that my world was unravelling in front of my eyes, and most people are the same. Give people time and space to find the words they need to convey their experience. Sometimes they may be so numb and overwhelmed with grief that the only thing they are able to do is sit and stare at a wall. In those moments, all they need is for you to sit and stare at the wall with them.

People crave normality and often want to do normal everyday things without fear of judgement. If everyone surrounding those bereaved recognises the loss, it means the individual/couple/family can focus on grieving, rather than utilising their small reserves of energy to defend their right to grieve.

Finally, remember that when a pet dies it is not only a story of pain; there is also beauty in the ashes.

10. What words would you whisper into a bereaved person's ear today?

Maybe today you are looking at people on Instagram or Facebook, or at others in your life, and thinking, 'How? How on earth have they got to the stage in life where they are happy? How have they run the race and are still here to tell the tale?' Well, let me reassure you of something.

I had no clue how I was going to get to the finish line. I didn't even know how I was going to get over the starting line, but I just kept stepping forwards and, before I knew it,

I was on my way. So, I am here to cheer you on and be that small voice you need to hear telling you, 'You can do this and you will survive.'

'The dog has been esteemed and loved by all the people on earth and he has deserved this affection for he renders services that have made him man's best friend.'

Alfred Barbou

APPENDIX 2

Thirty-One Days of Grief Support and Journalling Prompts to Help You Navigate the Next Month

DAY 1

❋ ❋

Wanting to hide away following any type of loss is totally normal. It doesn't mean you are having a breakdown or have suddenly developed a panic disorder; it simply means you need time out, and want to use that time to process what you have just experienced. So be gentle with yourself. Allow the tears to fall, eat chocolate, eat comforting soup, do whatever you need to do to get you through the darkest days of grief.

TASK FOR THE DAY

Write here or in your journal how you feel. Be honest. Be raw. This is your space to process your feelings with no fear of judgement.

_____

_____

_____

_____

_____

_____

_____

_____

_____

_____

DAY 2

* *

Today is about self-care. It is normal not to want to look after yourself following any type of loss, but I urge you to ignore the desire to forget you, because *you* matter. Often people see little purpose in eating well, or trying to rest, and not doing these things can almost feel like an act of self-expression, as if you are showing the world that life is too hard and you want to give up. But it is essential that you do look after yourself, so do it for you and do it in honour of the pet you have lost.

TASK FOR THE DAY

Do at least one or two of the following (or why not do all of them!).

* Shower.
* Find your most favourite item of clothing and wear it.
* What do you love to eat? Cook it or buy it.
* What is your favourite movie? Watch it.
* What is your favourite book? Dig it out and reread it.
* Who is your favourite person to chat with? Call them.

Today is about you. Today is about acknowledging you matter and your pain matters.

DAY 3

* *

Many of us are taught to put pain into a nice, neat parcel and hide it away. We are encouraged by society to put on a brave face and get on with life, and this is even more true when it comes to grief connected to animals. While we do need to carry on – our bills still need to be paid, so we can keep a roof over our heads – we definitely should not be encouraged to run from pain. Sometimes we just need to yield to the tears and immerse ourselves in our feelings and emotions so we can process them. Once they are processed and our brain has reluctantly come to terms with the sad loss we have faced, the healing can commence.

TASK FOR THE DAY

What do you feel society is saying to you about your loss? Write down five messages you are hearing from those around you. Now consider if these are helpful to you. If they aren't helpful, consider how you should respond and move forwards.

1 _____

2 _____

3 _____

4 _____

5 _____

DAY 4

We all have dreams and we all have a vision of how our life should look. Loss doesn't take these hopes and plans into account, it just rips them up in front of our eyes.

I think one of the key parts of grief is accepting that, in the briefest of moments, life changed forever, so that it no longer resembles what we had planned or hoped for. This means processing the shock, accepting the painful reality of life now being different, and then being willing to consider a new plan and a different future. None of this is easy – in fact it is incredibly difficult – but once we have considered a new way forwards it makes life feel a little more stable and back under control.

TASK FOR THE DAY

What three things would help you move forwards? Do you need to consider getting another pet? Do you need to create a memorial space for your pet? Do you need to spend less time on social media, and more time enjoying nature? Do you need to find someone you can chat with about your loss?

1 _____

2 _____

3 _____

DAY 5

* *

Friends can be such a great support when you are going through any form of loss. Of course, there can be the odd person who isn't the greatest at emotional support, but there are also often unexpected treasures, people you never thought would show up in your moment of need who blow you away with their kindness. I always say grief is the ultimate life sieve – it reveals what matters and shows you people's true characters. While this sieve can unearth some potential issues, it can also make life so much richer for you in the future, so try to embrace it and not fear it.

TASK FOR THE DAY

Which of your friends have been a support to you? Have any of your friends surprised you with their kindness and love? Write down three things that have been true gifts to you, so you never forget them.

1 _____

2 _____

3 _____

DAY 6

Many people worry that they shouldn't talk of the animal they have lost. They fear others may think they aren't coping, or are wallowing in misery, or perhaps even seeking attention. Oh, how untrue these things are. Talking of the pet you have lost does nothing more than show the world you care deeply. I have repeatedly said throughout this book that talking is key, and that's only because it is so true that people don't need to hear this message only once, they need to hear it over and over again, so they feel encouraged to do it. I urge you to keep talking about your feelings, keep talking about the grief, so your brain can start to accept the loss.

TASK FOR THE DAY

Write down what you want the world to know about the animal you have sadly lost.

_____

_____

_____

_____

_____

_____

_____

_____

DAY 7

When I hear people say they are fighting back the tears, my first question is always: 'Why?' Let me encourage you to weep whenever you need to. Sob on the floor. Let your tears help you to feel the pain, and to let it pass.

TASK FOR THE DAY

Go to a private place where you fear no judgement and let the tears flow. Don't let that inner voice tell you not to go there in case you can't stop once you have started; this will just keep you locked in the pain. Cry. Release the pain, which will in turn release the hormones and chemicals that tears of grief contain. Expect to feel drained following a release of powerful emotion, so ensure you have the time to recompose yourself, or a time to rest or even sleep.

DAY 8

I don't know if you are like me, but I fear looking weak, and worry that people may think I am not coping. This was a real stumbling block when I lost Jake. I think it is odd that these worries even enter our minds, and maybe that's a society issue? Or perhaps it's due to how we were raised, for instance if we have been conditioned to think of others before we consider what is actually best for our own well-being? Whatever the reason, there comes a time when we need to forget what others think and be true to ourselves. When we fight conformity and embrace true self-expression, amazing things can happen – not only can we begin to heal, we also give others the freedom to be true to themselves.

TASK FOR THE DAY

Do you feel you act in a certain way due to societal pressure or because those around you have told you to conform? Do you feel you would be happier and more at peace if you acted differently from these expectations? If the answer is yes, consider how you can make changes. Going through loss can blow your world to pieces, and sometimes this gives you the chance to make real changes as your life starts to be rebuilt. You don't need to put all the pieces back into the same place!

DAY 9

* *

People often ask me when the 'missing them' will end. The answer is simple: never! Sometimes this makes me feel like the bearer of bad news, but it is actually a gift. Why would anyone want the 'missing them' to end? If you didn't miss them, it would mean you were glad they had left, and of course you would never feel like that. For me, the 'missing them' shows the world that I loved them endlessly. It shows that they left a space in my life that can never and should never be filled by any other pet or person, as only they can fit that exact space. It also shows one other important thing: they mattered then, they matter now and they will always matter.

TASK FOR THE DAY

Try to rewire your thinking. The world tells us that missing animals is wrong, and we need to move on and get over it. It tells us that missing a pet is a curse rather than a blessing. As long as we feel a need to fight our natural feelings, we will resent having these feelings present in our life, and this can become a source of conflict in our minds. If we can change our thinking and accept that it's a gift and a blessing to miss a pet that has died, we can find room for these feelings in our life, and naturally adjust to them. Once we accept it's normal and right to feel this way, we also leave no room for feelings of shame and guilt. If you can

untangle what you have been taught and accept this new
way of thinking, it can be life-changing.

DAY 10

* *

Grief and loss bring chaos. It is like our lives are put into a washing machine and all hell breaks loose when it's whizzing around in circles. Everything in that machine changes shape. Dye leaks out of items and runs into others. It's important to recognise this part of loss, as fresh grief can trigger past pain. If you have been through previous trauma or have encountered past loss, losing your pet may open up unresolved issues for you. If this is happening to you, please don't be scared. Find a counsellor who can help you talk about your feelings and unwrap complex emotions.

TASK FOR THE DAY

Can you think of different ways you can express your grief? Write a list of ways you could express the pain you are feeling, which would help you move through the grieving process.

1 _____

2 _____

3 _____

4 _____

DAY 11

What happens if you can't cry? What happens if the tears just won't flow? Well, don't panic. Sometimes the shock of loss prevents tears from being able to come. A lack of tears does not mean you didn't love your pet and it certainly doesn't mean you didn't care. Everyone is different, and for some their natural response may not be to weep on the floor; it may be to write a song, or run a marathon. Grief can be expressed in so many different ways and is as personal as your fingerprint. So, the only important thing is finding your way to express your grief so that it can be channelled and processed.

TASK FOR THE DAY

Write a letter to your pet telling them how it felt when they entered your life.

_____

_____

_____

_____

_____

_____

_____

_____

_____

DAY 12

How can a person feel this much pain? This is a question I would often ask myself, especially in the dark hours of the night when I felt scared due to the amount of pain I was experiencing. The hurt felt like a giant before me, and the thought of continuing forwards with this pain looming over me was beyond daunting. I simply didn't understand how it could be so great and so consuming . . . and then I had a light bulb moment – the pain was this huge and unending because the love I felt for the one I had lost was unlimited. With unlimited love comes unlimited pain when the pet or the person we adore dies. This realisation stopped me questioning it, and I accepted it for what it was – and when I stopped fighting the pain, it became less scary. It stopped being an enemy and became a silent companion, until it was time for it to start to leave my life, leaving only the love behind in its wake.

TASK FOR THE DAY

How would you explain loss? Write down how you explain your loss to someone. Sometimes verbalising our pain helps.

_____

_____

_____

DAY 13

* *

I love the spring. It feels like it's the start of warmer days and longer evenings. However, I didn't always feel like this. When I was grieving, every month was bleak. Seasons blended into one another, and the forecast was always terrifying. So how did this change? Well, it certainly didn't happen overnight! But one day I could see a shoot of new life pushing through the ground, and eventually that turned into the tiniest of flowers. New life and brighter outlooks don't happen as quickly as we may like. Seeds have to be sown and the ground needs to be ready – but then, without any warning, growth starts to happen. The ground starts to move and one tiny bud springs forth. This is enough to give us hope that tomorrow may be brighter, and that life may be worth embracing after all.

TASK FOR THE DAY

Write down what gives you hope that tomorrow may be brighter. What brings you joy, what can bring a smile to your face in the darkest of days?

_____

_____

_____

_____

_____

DAY 14

* *

I don't think we can ever prepare for the loss of a pet. We can certainly start grieving before the death happens – if our pet is very ill, for instance – but that is very different from actually preparing for the trapdoor to open, just in case it does. If we try to prepare, we just rob ourselves of experiencing true joy in the moment.

So often people say to me, 'If only I hadn't made as many plans then it wouldn't hurt as much now.' While it is natural to feel like this, it is not accurate, as the pain of loss is just as huge whether you had made plans or not; but one way you experienced the happiness and excitement of dreaming of future adventures, and the other way you just felt the anticipation of pain and grief.

Your brain may try to encourage you to be more pessimistic in future, and to expect a life of loss, as a form of self-protection. I am a strong believer that this helps no one, and just means you are then faced with a life of less hope, less peace and less joy. Hold on to hope with both hands. Celebrate every ounce of happiness that lands in your lap, and try to remain as positive as possible about the future. If you sadly need to face loss again, you will deal with it then, but at least you have had seasons of blissful joy.

TASK FOR THE DAY

Try to write a poem or find a quote about the pain you are feeling. If you allow yourself to express your pain creatively, it can help transform it.

_____
_____
_____
_____
_____
_____
_____
_____
_____
_____
_____
_____
_____
_____
_____
_____
_____
_____
_____
_____
_____

DAY 15

* *

Today is a day for dealing with guilt. With most forms of grief, guilt comes as part of the package. For many when they have lost a pet the grief lies in decisions surrounding treatment or about selecting euthanasia. Constant questions torment: Could we have done more? If I had noticed something earlier would it have been more treatable? Should we have selected a different treatment plan? Should we have given them more time to recover? Could we have prevented the accident?

A million questions, with a million variable answers, and none of them help remove the pain of grief and loss. We have to get to a place of accepting we made the best choices with the information available to us. We have to accept we didn't have a crystal ball to see into the future: all we had was the information in front of us, and every choice was made with the best intentions and with love at the heart of it. We have to lay down the 'what if's' and accept 'what was'. It is in this acceptance that peace can be found and grief can continue to be processed.

TASK FOR THE DAY

Is there a special place you associate with your pet? Maybe a walk you would regularly go on together? Perhaps the place you first chose your pet to come home with you? It can be hard to return to special places after loss, but it can also be incredibly healing. The longer a person leaves it to return, the harder it can become, and sometimes people even become scared or phobic of revisiting. Can I encourage you to take a friend's hand and venture back to that place? If you need to cry, cry. If you feel led to share memories, good or bad, do so.

DAY 16

* *

I had been through so much loss, people used to tell me I was brave not to give up, but do you want to know the truth? I did: a hundred times a day, thousands of times a week, I gave up. I screamed, I yelled and sobbed, saying, 'That's it, I am done.' When Jake died the pain overwhelmed me and I was fed up with being broken, down on my knees. So, if you are kicking yourself for giving up, please know this: *everyone* gives up. When the pain is all-consuming and life feels like it has lost its meaning, we all scream at the sky and shout, 'I can't take any more!' In that moment, we discover that life carries on regardless of whether we have the strength to continue or not, and all we need to do is sit for a while and wait for a fresh wave of courage to refuel us for the next part of the journey.

TASK FOR THE DAY

There is something extremely cathartic in screaming at the sky, in shouting and releasing that internal pain. If you can find a place where you can go to scream, holler, wail and release some of the pain, do it today. Why not go to the gym and put on a pair of boxing gloves and hit a punchbag? Or just punch a pillow in your bedroom. Physical acts can truly help emotional pain.

DAY 17

People often say, 'You will conquer this grief,' as if it's an obstacle course you have to negotiate. But no one conquers grief; it is something you have to face, not fight. It can't be skipped over and it can't be defeated. You have to allow it to surround you like fog on a mountain top, and only when the fog rises will you see the path in front of you. It is not the enemy, even though it often feels like it. It is most certainly a giant – but it's a giant made out of love, pain, lessons, gentleness and a million other emotions. If we welcome the giant around the table, and don't try to make it stay on the other side of the door, it can teach us so much about ourselves and the world.

TASK FOR THE DAY

How would you describe grief? What does this giant look like in your life?

_____

_____

_____

_____

_____

_____

_____

_____

DAY 18

People often used to remind me how many pets die every day, as if that would make me feel better. While it was useful to be reminded that I wasn't the only person in the world going through loss, knowing others were battling grief didn't make my pain any less; it just made me acutely aware of how many bereaved people there were.

It is strange to me how people like to minimise the pain of losing a pet, but I want to assure you that even if those around you don't acknowledge the gravity of your loss, I do. I know your heart is broken right now. I know no words I can offer will take that pain away from you. But sometimes it is enough to know our pain has been seen, and our loss has been recognised.

TASK FOR THE DAY

I want you to fill the box on the following page with all the words you feel right now. Write them simply, or write them in different sizes and different colours.

DAY 19

* *

'What do you need?'

I was asked this so many times when walking through grief following the loss of pets and people I loved. I often had no clue what I needed; my mind was overwhelmed and flooded with emotion. Sometimes I felt utterly numb, at other times a million different emotions consumed me.

There were many occasions when I couldn't have conducted a conversation, but I still wanted to be with people, as I felt so lost and scared by the feelings I was trying to process. At those times I was only capable of sitting and staring at the wall, and I just needed someone to sit and stare at the wall with me. I wish I had been able to tell people that.

TASK FOR THE DAY

Think about what you need. If you can't find the words in the moment, perhaps take some time to write it down, and then give it to your friends and family to read. It can be incredibly hard to support someone through grief, and just giving people some pointers can be a huge help to them, but also to yourself down the line.

_____

_____

_____

_____

DAY 20

* *

Grief has so many layers. After losing your pet, it's obvious that you will be grieving for the animal you have lost, but it may surprise you that you could also be grieving over many other things simultaneously. One of the big things I grieved over was losing my joy. One day I was beyond happy, the next day I was beyond crushed, and I couldn't even imagine a time when I would smile again. I grieved that I no longer cared about normal everyday things. Loss made these simple things feel irrelevant, even though they had previously brought me such joy.

TASK FOR THE DAY

Write down what you think you are grieving for besides the loss of your beloved pet.

_____

_____

_____

_____

_____

_____

_____

_____

_____

DAY 21

It is very common when you are grieving to feel you are spending your life apologising for things that just flew out of your mouth. Grief seems to remove a filter, and without even meaning to be rude you may have found yourself saying the most awful things to the people around you. People often say to me, 'Maybe it would be easier if I walked around with a sign saying "I'm sorry", as I seem to offend people without even trying.' So, if you feel this, know you are not alone. When you are trying to process pain and deal with loss, it is very difficult to control your emotions and your tongue, and one of the horrible side effects of this is sadly putting your foot in it on a regular basis. So just be honest, be willing to apologise, and ask for grace from the people who love you.

TASK FOR THE DAY

Take 15 minutes to do something just for you. Whether it be reading a book, soaking in the bath, enjoying a coffee while looking at your garden – whatever you choose to do today, these minutes are your minutes and I hope they bring a smile to your face.

DAY 22

* *

The world often tells us that one loss is way worse than another, but the truth is that all loss is relative to a person's life and experience. Society has no right to compare losses or determine how much a person should or shouldn't grieve, but it sadly does this all the time. I find this grief hierarchy extraordinarily hard to understand; I simply refuse to accept it, and will spend my life fighting it. Loss is loss. Grief is grief. Someone's age doesn't denote their worth or their place in this world. Likewise, whether a person is grieving the loss of a human or an animal is irrelevant to the support they may need or the pain they may feel.

No one has the right to diminish your grief or your pain, or tell you how your loss was less important or notable than another's. There should be no hierarchy in grief.

TASK FOR THE DAY

Write a letter to your pet telling them all the ways they helped you and brought you joy.

_____

_____

_____

_____

_____

_____

DAY 23

* *

How often have we been told not to cry, or perhaps how many times have we told others not to cry? Society doesn't allow much space for weeping; we have been taught wrongly that to be strong means showing no or very little emotion. We can accept the odd pretty tear falling down a person's cheek, and may even be touched at seeing it before us, but it's different if someone is sobbing hysterically at our feet. If we are the one weeping, it feels messy, ugly and out of control. If we are the ones witnessing it, it can make us feel helpless and inept at dealing with such visible distress.

But this is where we have gone wrong as humans. Emotion, *all* emotion, is what makes us human; we should welcome the heart-wrenching sobs as much as we welcome the belly-doubling hysterical laughs. Life is amazing, but it can also be utterly crap. It can be beautiful and so very ugly. It can bring unending joy and endless pain. But we survive it by embracing every moment, by allowing ourselves and others to express it all – whether that be by weeping an ocean of tears, or by laughing till tears of joy roll down our cheeks.

TASK FOR THE DAY

It's another crying day. Let the tears roll. Tears of grief and sadness are composed of a different substance from tears of joy – how amazing is that? They contain hormones and chemicals, and it is essential we let them out so they can't cause damage to us emotionally and/or physically. So be kind to yourself and let them flow today. It may help to put on a piece of music, or go into the shower.

DAY 24

* *

How can you let go of a pet you have truly loved? I wish there was a trick to make this easier, but sadly there isn't. It will never be easy letting go of anything you have dearly loved, but then I don't think it should be easy. It should be gut-wrenching, it should be a battle, it should tear our hearts apart. Loss should be incomprehensible and bring us to our knees. That pain shows the love. Those tears reveal the heartbreak. And while we have to let go physically of the pet we adore, they will never leave our hearts, our minds, our lives. All those memories, all those magical moments, will live on in your heart forever.

If yesterday you ran from the pain, but today you sit with the pain, and tomorrow you face the pain . . . that, my friend, is the journey to healing a broken heart. So don't panic. Don't feel you should be further along the path than you currently are. You are doing fine. You don't need to walk at someone else's speed. You don't need to fret if people make you feel you are healing too slowly; that is their issue, not yours.

Your loss. Your pain. Your walk.

TASK FOR THE DAY

Use this space to write down the misconceptions you feel surrounding your loss.

_____

_____

_____

_____

_____

_____

_____

_____

_____

_____

_____

_____

_____

_____

_____

_____

_____

_____

_____

_____

_____

_____

_____

_____

_____

_____

_____

DAY 25

Feeling guilt over grieving is super-common, whether that be over a pet or a person. It is hard to carry grief when we feel guilt for bringing sadness to the table. If all those present want you to just be happy and look at the brighter side of life, and then you come along with swollen eyes and tear-soaked tissues, whatever is or isn't said, you can quickly feel awful for changing the tone of the conversation or for lowering the positive energy. Over time this guilt can build and most bereaved people will withdraw themselves from the table, or even the house, because the weight of the guilt on top of the grief is just too much.

If you are the bereaved person, I want to encourage you to fight this guilt and show up anyway. This urge to protect others can at times magnify your pain, and however much we want to conceal sadness from our loved ones, your priority is your own well-being.

For those who are supporting the bereaved and are sitting around that table, I urge you to constantly reassure the grieving person that it's okay to bring their tears and pain to every meal. Make them know it's a safe place, and no guilt is needed, as this will help them on their walk to healing.

TASK FOR THE DAY

Are you carrying guilt over the death of your pet? List the things you feel guilty about, and then decide how you can lay down that guilt and walk into freedom.

_____
_____
_____
_____
_____
_____
_____
_____
_____
_____
_____
_____
_____
_____
_____
_____
_____
_____
_____
_____
_____
_____
_____
_____
_____

DAY 26

Feeling lonely is horrible and most people who have lost a pet will tell you that they feel desperately lonely at times. This happens for two reasons: firstly, because they have lost their faithful companion from their side; secondly, grieving is such a solitary experience. When walking through grief, a person will often feel like they are the only person on the planet enduring that pain. There is no magic cure, but there are a few tips I can offer if you are trying to get used to a silent house.

* It may help to invite someone to stay for a while, or perhaps to just regularly visit.
* Consider leaving music playing on the radio each day, just so you get to hear other voices and to eliminate the silence.
* Call people daily on the phone so you have some personal interaction.
* Try to leave the house as often as possible; human interaction can help with the feeling of loneliness.

TASK FOR THE DAY

Write a letter to your pet saying goodbye and explaining how you now feel without them here.

_____

_____

_____

_____

_____

_____

_____

_____

_____

_____

_____

_____

_____

_____

_____

_____

_____

_____

_____

_____

_____

_____

_____

_____

_____

_____

DAY 27

* *

Have you ever cried for so long you are scared? Scared you will never stop weeping? Scared that this is how life will look forever? Scared that you will never smile again? This fear is so normal; it is okay to acknowledge it, and it helps to discuss it. When grief grips your soul, it feels bleak and desolate, and this lack of hope for a brighter tomorrow is part of the grieving process. I promise you the sun will rise and this scary, black grief will lessen.

Try not to even consider what tomorrow has in store when you feel the terror take hold; just focus on today. If today seems too much to handle, just get through the next hour. Whether you take massive steps forwards, or the tiniest micro-steps, it doesn't matter; progress is being made – and you, my friend, are going to make it through.

TASK FOR THE DAY

Saying goodbye to the body of your pet is so incredibly hard. Maybe for you that will take place at the vet's; perhaps it will be on a hillside as you scatter their ashes. Wherever and whenever it is, it will be a moment that lives with you forever. To come to terms with that process, I want to encourage you to talk about the event. By talking about it, you allow your brain to accept what has happened and eventually, over time, you may feel more at peace.

DAY 28

* *

Broken hearts continue to beat. Now, I see this as a good thing, but when I was broken it was the last thing I wanted to hear. I didn't want my heart to carry on beating, I wanted to be saved from the pain. So, if that's how you feel today, I want you to know that it's to be expected.

There is a phrase commonly bandied about that I used to hate with a passion: 'Time heals all wounds'. Is it correct? No, time doesn't automatically heal all wounds, but it is possible for the wounds to no longer bleed. And, yes, that does happen over time and can't be fast-forwarded. Gradually your grief muscles also get stronger and more adept at carrying the pain, so the grief you are feeling becomes more manageable over time. So, while I wish I could speed up time for you, I sadly can't, and I just hope you can believe me when I say this: it will get easier.

You are going to make it through this black tunnel. Just hold on.

TASK FOR THE DAY

Do you feel you have any wounds that are unhealed from your past that are possibly being triggered by your current pet loss? If yes, what are they and how do you think you can work on processing this unresolved trauma?

DAY 29

* *

I wish the world would recognise and acknowledge that one pet can never replace another. Also, that grieving in no way shows a lack of gratitude for another pet or person. Pain and joy, tears and smiles, even regret and thankfulness can easily sit alongside one another, so don't let anyone tell you any different. You can feel it all. In the same hour you can scream and laugh. You can feel helpless and hopeful. You can want to die and want to live. This is what grieving looks like: a consortium of opposing feelings in one mind, in one body. You are normal to feel it all.

TASK FOR THE DAY

How would you describe your grief today? Has it changed shape over the past few weeks?

_____

_____

_____

_____

_____

_____

_____

_____

_____

_____

DAY 30

Loss is often made up of 'if onlys'. If only I had spent more time with them. If only I had taken them to see the vet earlier. If only I had chosen a different treatment plan.

I used to constantly wonder how I would ever find peace with so many questions and regrets. I thought I was destined to live in turmoil and have a constant internal conflict, but I was wrong. I found peace with not knowing and peace with accepting that I can't change the past. That doesn't mean I still wouldn't love to know all the answers; it just means I learned to accept that I can't. There wasn't a magical moment when this peace arrived, and it wasn't something I did that made it happen. Over time I just gradually became accustomed to living with the unknowns and accepting that the past can't be altered, and that brought with it a feeling of being okay to live with a million question marks and an acceptance that I did the best I could given the circumstances. I hope if you wrestle with questions and internal conflict that one day you too will find peace.

TASK FOR THE DAY

Write the letter you would send to a friend who is grieving, offering all the advice you can think of. After you have written it, sit and look at how much of that advice you are following yourself.

_____
_____
_____
_____
_____
_____
_____
_____
_____
_____
_____
_____
_____
_____
_____
_____
_____
_____
_____
_____
_____
_____
_____
_____
_____
_____
_____
_____

DAY 31

When we are young, we are usually taught how to articulate joy and happiness, but we are rarely taught the language of loss. How do you even begin to express earth-shattering pain? How do you explain to those around you the depth of heartache you are experiencing?

I just wanted people to understand that my world was unravelling in front of my eyes, and however much I begged for the pain to stop, it didn't. But I couldn't find the words in my fog of grief to tell them anything other than, 'I am hurting.'

If you feel like this, please know you are not alone, and as you emerge from the fog of pain you will feel better equipped to explain how you feel.

TASK FOR THE DAY

What are you struggling to express to those around you? Use this space to try to verbalise what you want the world to know.

_____

_____

_____

_____

_____

_____

_____